T0063481

FERTILIZER 'TWEEN MY TOES

An Autobiography

The true story of a country boy from South Georgia who found fame and a little bit of fortune in radio stations and country music, after his teen years of getting cow manure 'tween his toes.

MARSHALL ROWLAND

iUniverse LLC
Bloomington

FERTILIZER 'TWEEN MY TOES

iUniverse books may be ordered through booksellers or by contacting:

iUniverse
1663 Liberty Drive
Bloomington, IN 47403
www.iuniverse.com
1-800-Authors (1-800-288-4677)

Because of the dynamic nature of the Internet, any web addresses or links contained in this book may have changed since publication and may no longer be valid. The views expressed in this work are solely those of the author and do not necessarily reflect the views of the publisher, and the publisher hereby disclaims any responsibility for them.

Any people depicted in stock imagery provided by Thinkstock are models, and such images are being used for illustrative purposes only. Certain stock imagery © Thinkstock.

ISBN: 978-1-4917-1570-3 (sc)
ISBN: 978-1-4917-1571-0 (e)

Library of Congress Control Number: 2013921362

Printed in the United States of America.

iUniverse rev. date: 11/20/2013

Special thanks to my four sons—Marty, Ricky, Brian, and Stephen—and to my special friends J. C. Hunnicutt, Russell Baze, and Judy Johnson, and all the others who prompted me to take on this task. To them I say thanks for making me dig up all those pleasant (and a few unpleasant) memories, many I thought I had forgotten.

Also, to anyone who feels I've stepped on their toes or written incorrectly about them, I want to apologize in advance. As I write this, I have been on this earth for eighty-two years, and I've had to do a lot of mind searching to bring things up from the past in order to put it down on paper. There may be some slight inaccuracies, and if so, I apologize for those errors. To anyone I may have hurt, overlooked, or offended in any way, please accept my sincerest apologies.

For those of you who have comments, please contact the author at marshallwrowland@gmail.com.

This book is not written in chronological order due to the fact that certain important events were all happening at the same time. I have included all of the more interesting facts of my life.

CONTENTS

CHAPTER 1

MY EARLY SOUTH GEORGIA YEARS

I feel it's important as you read a book with a title like *Fertilizer 'tween My Toes* to know that it's all based upon my unusual up-bringing and the success I have achieved despite the hardships of my childhood. I often say that I'm the most blessed man on earth, and as you read my story you'll understand why I feel that way.

I was born in Brunswick, Georgia, on January 23, 1931. My parents were John Alexander and Chloe Francis Rowland. There were six children in my family: three older brothers, one older sister, and a younger brother, Bobby. I never saw my oldest brother, Ed. They told me he had run away from home before I was born and was living his life in California. My older sister Dorothy died when I was only two or three years old from double pneumonia. During the early years of my life, that left only me and my two older brothers, John and Paul.

My younger brother Bobby, or Robert, was born when I was three and a half years old. After his birth, they took our mother away from us, and she was placed in an asylum or an institution in Milledgeville, Georgia, where she would remain until she died many years later. I was eventually told that she had lost her mind during childbirth.

The only memory I have of my mother is of the day when three policemen came and took her away in a small automobile. They did so because she had broken into a big house across the street from where we lived and was being uncontrollable. She and the driver were inside the auto and the two policemen stood on the running board as it drove away from our house. Without a doubt, that lone memory of my mother being taken away when I was so young has gone through my mind thousands of times over eight decades.

Shortly thereafter, Daddy's sister, my aunt Polly, came down from Greenville, South Carolina, to see that we were taken care of. She was a practical nurse and decided it was best since Bobby was a newborn infant that he should go to Miami, Florida, and live with my mother's sister. John, Paul, and I were to remain in Brunswick, and Daddy would get a housekeeper to look after us. That housekeeper turned out to be Mrs. Achsa Leggett, who over time would be the closest thing to a mother as I would ever know in my lifetime.

Soon after that, John moved out of the house and in with some friends of his, the Norman Highsmith family. He would live with them and finish high school at Glynn Academy. That left Paul, me, and Mrs. Leggett living in the big house in Brunswick, because Daddy traveled away following his work in construction. He was a building supervisor and once told me that during World War I he went behind the troops building small hospitals to care for the wounded.

Mrs. Leggett was married to a fellow named Dave, and he always had a wine bottle in his back pocket. In fact, I saw him very few times when he wasn't drinking. He would visit Mrs. Leggett on many occasions while we lived in Brunswick.

At some point, my father started drinking heavily and quit sending money home to our housekeeper to pay the rent and for groceries and our other living expenses. Even though I was a small child, I remember one day when we were served with an eviction notice by a police officer. I also remember about that time some people coming from the county to our house and talking to Mrs. Leggett about an orphanage for me and Paul.

Since our housekeeper couldn't or didn't know how to contact Daddy or perhaps didn't know what to do, she got in touch with Aunt Polly, who made the bus trip back to Brunswick. Together they decided that rather than an orphanage, it would be best for us to move out into the country, where Mrs. Leggett had two old-maid sisters who owned a little country store in Waynesville, about twenty-five miles away. Until that time, I had never been away from Brunswick, and in reality I had no idea of what was to be the future for me and Paul. I suppose that as a child of six years old by that time, I was worried about what was going to happen to me, who would feed and clothe me.

Arrangements were made, and we moved out to a rural area that was all new to me. Living conditions in the Waynesville community were much different from what we had in Brunswick. There was no running water, no electricity, and no toilets like we had in the city. Mrs. Leggett's two old-maid sisters were Miss Lilla and Miss Lula.

The house we moved into was located right next to the Atlantic Coast Line Railroad, and it had four big rooms, each with a fireplace. It had a smaller attached dining room with a kitchen to the rear. Right out back was the chicken yard, where they could throw food scraps to feed the chickens. Mrs. Leggett and Miss Lilla slept in one of the big back bedrooms, and Miss Lula slept alone in the other. Even though Miss Lilla owned the grocery store, all of them—including Dave—participated in running it. Dave would open the store each morning around seven o'clock and keep the little money he took in from sales on his shift so that later during the day he could buy his supply of wine.

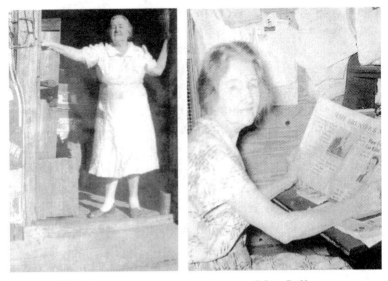

Mrs. Leggett   **Miss Lilla**

While we lived in Waynesville, the ladies insisted that Paul and I take a bath at least once a week, whether we needed it or not. Sometimes in winter, the pumped water in the washtub was so cold, you could bathe yourself all over in less than a minute—you either splashed fast or froze. Our toilet was an outhouse. Not a normal one with a half moon on the door, but one with four holes in it and no half moon. The smaller holes were reserved for the ladies, and they were marked with a Sears Roebuck catalog, while the other two were for males and were marked with a Montgomery Ward catalog. Those catalogs served as our toilet paper.

For a short time, we had a tent theater that had moved from Woodbine, Georgia. The owner, Mr. Miller, would show us movies twice a week. For only ten cents, we got to see the movies—mostly Westerns, or cowboy oaters, but occasionally an exciting Tarzan movie.

I will never forget June 8, 1938. I was only seven years old, barefooted with overalls on, playing at the old water pump between the house and the store. It intrigued me that cool water would come up out of the ground by just pumping on the handle. Cool water in the summertime was always welcome.

Suddenly, I heard someone call me from nearby. When I looked up, there was my aunt Polly who had come to see us. Mrs. Leggett was standing nearby, and between them stood a little boy dressed in a sunsuit and wearing a frilly pleated shirt, with fancy shoes and socks. Today I would describe him as looking like Little Lord Fauntleroy. My immediate thought was, *What is this little squirt doing here?*

Seeing how puzzled I was, Aunt Polly spoke up and said, "Marshall, this is your little brother Bobby." Aunt Polly had gone to Miami and gotten him to come and live with me and Paul in the country. I was very excited to see him, even though he was three years younger than me. It seems everyone in the community immediately took a liking to little Bobby, who was only four years old when he arrived. It didn't take him long to learn country ways, and never again would he wear those city clothes that he had worn from Miami on that eventful day.

Mrs. Leggett's husband, Dave, really loved Bobby and spent a lot of time with him. He called him "spring frog Isaac," and that name would stick with Bobby as long as he lived in Waynesville. I always thought Bobby had more friends than I did, because he was younger and seemed to be eager to make new friends.

Even though I was only six-and-half years old when we moved from Brunswick, I was already in the second grade at Sydney Lanier grammar school there. The little school in Waynesville only had three rooms, with two or three grades in each. My teacher was Miss Julia Wiggins, and she realized immediately that I was doing the same thing in the second grade in Brunswick as they were now doing in the third grade in her classes. So she promptly moved me over one row in the seating, jumping me from the second to the third grade in one year. I suppose that was why I would go on to graduate a year younger than others in my class.

While we were living in Waynesville, a traveling preacher pitched a tent and held a week-long Holy Ghost Revival. I went one night out of curiosity. I suppose I just wanted to know what a revival was all about. I was really shocked when one of his assistants came down the aisle and grabbed me and dragged me up to the altar, where the preacher beat me on my head and yelled out all kinds of religious chants. In later years, I figured he did that in order to get others to come forward so maybe they would put some money in his collection plate. Apparently I was his guinea pig.

For a few days after that, some of my buddies shied away from me because they thought I was different, since I had now been "saved." After a few more days, though, everything got back to normal. From that time on until I married my wife, I never attended church regularly, nor did I care to join a church because of that event. It was hard to get it out of my mind.

While all these Waynesville events were taking place in my life, World War II had started, and every evening people would gather in the little grocery store to listen to the battery radio for news of the war. At night we could see the searchlights streaming up into the air from Fort Stewart, Georgia, a military base many miles away. Everyone listened avidly to Walter Winchell or Douglas Edwards as they reported the events going on overseas. It became a nightly gathering spot for the little town of no more than seventy-five people. I seriously doubt that many of the townsfolk even had a radio. At that time, many of the young men around Waynesville went off to the service, and some of them would never return.

Sometime after the war had started, another exciting event happened in our community: Okefenokee Rural Electric Co-op was founded and brought electricity to the area. The store and our house were among the first in the area to get electricity, and thus we had one of the most brightly lit houses around. No more trying to read at night by the kerosene lamps.

People from out in the country would come to the store and stand and stare at the electric lights or listen to the new electric radio, or they would come just to see the new icebox—which was now called a refrigerator. Up on Highway 82, Mr. Norman McVeigh had installed a jukebox that had bright lights flashing and flickering with the music. People would come in from the countryside thinking it was a heater that played music, and they would try to warm their hands and bodies by standing in front of it. Truly, electricity arriving to the area was a monumental event.

One day when I was just ten years old, a stranger who was a friend of the ladies who owned the little store came to see them. I suppose out of sympathy for him, Mrs. Leggett invited him to stay the night. He accepted, and he was to sleep with me in one of the front bedrooms where I usually slept alone.

I could tell right off that he was different—a bum of sorts. He was wearing dirty clothes and apparently did not have a job. He was unshaven and had a bad smell or body odor. After I went to bed that night and fell asleep, I suddenly awoke and felt a hand feeling me all over my body. I began to cry and tremble with fear. At ten years old, I did not know what he was doing, but I didn't like it because I had never experienced anything like this before.

My crying and trembling did not stop him. I immediately moved over to the edge and tried to get out of the bed, but his arm was wrapped around my body. I finally broke loose and rolled over onto the floor. I stayed there on the floor until I felt it was safe to get up and get away. I went outside, where I stayed on the front porch trembling and crying until daylight.

The next morning, sleep-deprived and still shuddering with fear, I did not know whether to tell of this event or not. When sunrise finally came, I put on my clothes and left for school without eating or saying anything about what had happened or even saying good-bye. I think Mrs. Leggett may have suspected something.

Later in life, I finally I got over that traumatic event, and to this day I have only told a few close friends about it. The Bible teaches us that we should forgive others who do us wrong, but it took a long, long time for me, even as an adult, to forgive this stranger for what he attempted to do to me that night and to get it out of my mind. I never saw him again, and I will never forget that incident.

The fellow who had the most musical influence on me in my early years was Little Henry Wiggins. I met him when I was nine years old. Little Henry was blind in one eye and had gone to the blind school in Macon, Georgia. Even with only one eye, he was a great marble shooter and a good softball player. But most of all, he loved to play country music.

My early musical mentor and friend, on his only mode of transportation ... Little Henry Wiggins

Little Henry could play the piano, the mandolin, the guitar, and the fiddle. You name it and he could play it, yet he could not read music, I suppose because of his only having one eye. One time he told me he had music in his soul. He had learned to play by listening to the radio or phonograph records, and only improved when he went to the School for the Blind in Macon.

I was always attracted to Little Henry and his music. One day when I was twelve, I was listening to him play and sing. He and I were alone, and I casually picked up his guitar. He showed me some chords on it and how to keep rhythm. Within weeks, we were a duo, sitting on people's porches just playing and singing. Some folks, especially young kids, would sit on the railroad tracks out front as we sat on the porch and played until all hours of the evening.

Within weeks, we began going out in the nearby country area to people's houses. The war was raging overseas, and many local folks were glad to have some kind of entertainment. Most of them had no radio or other music, so the family would move all the furniture from the biggest room in the house where we would sit in one corner or in the hallway and play our hearts out while they danced. Little Henry insisted that as soon as they got on the floor to start dancing, we would stop playing our music and pass the hat for contributions.

That was the first money I ever made in my life. It gave me some insight, because I thought maybe there might be a future for me one day in country music—a chance I could play it or be associated with it in some way for a living. Little Henry had a huge collection of old 78 records by the early country music stars like Jimmie Rodgers, Bob Wills and the Texas Playboys, Hank Penny, Spade Cooley, and others. Plus he always talked about listening to the Saturday night Grand Ole Opry. We both got excited the night they introduced a new star on the Opry. His name was Ernest Tubb, and his band was called the Troubadours.

There I was at age twelve playing with Little Henry at dances in people's homes two or three times a month, making twenty to twenty-five dollars or sometimes more a month doing what I loved most: playing country music. Little Henry and I played together many, many times from that time on until I would leave him and the little town of Waynesville behind.

One day, while sitting on the second hole in the outhouse, I suddenly got the urge to order me a brand-new guitar from either the Sears Roebuck or the Montgomery Ward catalog. I ordered it COD without telling anyone. When it arrived a few days later from Sears, the train people just slowed down the train and threw the big box off, and it got all busted up. I was very saddened, but Mr. W. O. Beach, our postmaster, arranged for me to send it back.

Later they would send me a replacement, a beautiful white Silvertone guitar. This guitar was featured by Sears as part of their own line of musical instruments. For hours when I had nothing else to do, I would just sit and strum that beautiful guitar. Later I learned to whistle and play at the same time. Those were truly the good old days for me.

Every year, the local Baptist church would present a Christmas party for all the kids in the Waynesville area. They didn't have presents but instead gave out candy of all sorts and fruits and sometimes someone's leftover clothes. But they always had a brilliantly decorated, fresh-cut tree loaded with seemingly hundreds of twinkling lights.

Little Henry and I wore our best clean outfits, which were overalls, and we were sitting together admiring the tree when I said to him, "If you'll look at the tree while crossing your eyes, you'll see twice as many lights." He replied, "I can't, because I only have one eye." He and I were such good friends, I had forgotten about his having only one eye.

About the same time that Little Henry and I were playing for folks around the Waynesville area and I was busy improving my musical abilities, my older brother Paul got a job at the Gibson

Brothers Dairy about three miles outside Waynesville. Since I had nothing to do on many days after school during the week, I decided to go with him and help him, and sometimes he would give me a dime. After a few weeks went by, Paul got either lazy or smart and just sent me to do his work every weekday. At the end of the week, he would go and collect his money and pay me a small pittance.

After just two weeks had passed, Pete and Charles "Noody" Gibson—the brothers who owned the dairy—fired Paul and gave me the job full-time. I loved it. I could drink all the milk, buttermilk, and chocolate milk I wanted, and they paid me eight dollars a week. Every Saturday I got an extra dollar fifty when I would clean the cow milking stalls, clean out the barn, and shovel the cow manure. On the same day, I also cleaned out the pen or small lot where the thirty or forty cows were kept overnight. I would then shovel the fertilizer into a manure spreader, and the Gibson brothers would let me drive an old John Deere tractor all day long to haul it out and spread it into the fields.

I looked forward to this Saturday work because I got the thrill of driving the John Deere tractor around the barnyard for hours and hours. I would have probably shoveled the fertilizer for free just to get to drive that old tractor. For almost four years, every Saturday and sometimes on Sunday evening, I got plenty of fertilizer or cow manure 'tween my toes. Those were the happiest days of my life, and I would never forget them.

In 1945, when I was fourteen years old and had been working at the dairy for about two years, Pete Gibson suggested I get my driver's license so that if no one else was available, I could drive the milk truck to Brunswick and deliver the milk. I had already been driving it around the back roads to Waynesville on occasion. One Saturday morning when the sun was shining bright, I proudly drove the 1939 model Chevrolet milk truck down the main Highway 80 to Brunswick and went straight out to the Georgia Highway Patrol station north of town on US 17. I was somewhat apprehensive about getting a license and passing a driving test—to be honest, I was scared to death—but I sure was proud to be driving through town as a young kid.

The big, burly, heavyset, uniformed Georgia State Patrolman on duty saw me drive up in the old milk truck with Gibson Brothers Dairy painted on its side and didn't even test me. He just asked me a few gruff questions and then issued me a driver's license, since I had obviously driven in from the country without wrecking the truck or running over anyone. This occurred as the war was beginning to wind down, and I learned later that I'd obtained a license while only fourteen because working for the dairy was considered to be an essential occupation to the war effort at that time.

Sometimes I would want to pinch myself; I just couldn't get over the fact that I was now making almost a hundred dollars a month working at the dairy during the day and playing at night—and now, to top it off, I had my driver's license. People would stare at me sometimes when I drove by, not believing a kid of my age had such a job. Truly, I was on top of the world, in spite of the fertilizer I was getting 'tween my toes each Saturday.

At that time, I was very naive about city ways—such as how to look or ask for a restroom when I needed to relieve myself in the city. At the dairy, I simply went out back in the woods and did what comes naturally, and that was okay. At home with the four-hole outhouse, there was always an available hole. But one hot summer day while I was driving the milk truck making deliveries, I found myself right in downtown Brunswick at the main intersection on Newcastle and Gloucester streets when I had to find a restroom and find it fast.

I parked the truck right near the main intersection downtown. Beside me on the seat was a twelve-gauge shotgun that Noody Gibson had sent to town for a friend to be repaired. I took the barrel off the shotgun stock and then I cracked the passenger's side of the truck door barely ajar. Feeling secure that no one could see me, I stuck the barrel out of the crack in the door, and I urinated through it. What blessed relief it brought me. I did leave a little puddle on the street near the sidewalk, but I'm sure the sunshine took care of that in a few minutes.

When it comes to being naive, I probably could have won an award back in my early years. One Sunday morning I had to hitchhike back to Waynesville from Brunswick. The night before I had played at the casino on Saint Simons Island with Charles and Roy Oneal, with whom I spent the night shortly after getting my new steel guitar. I had caught a ride with a gentleman in a pickup truck out to Highway 17, where he dropped me off. I wasn't concerned; I felt sure I could get a ride on home to Waynesville so I could get back to my dairy work.

I was standing beside the highway with my guitar when a man driving a shiny new black 1947 Ford sedan stopped for me. It was one of the first new cars to be made right after the war. He stopped and asked me where I was headed, and when I told him Waynesville, he said, "Hop in. I'm going right past there."

As we drove, he kept asking me questions about who I was and all about my family or life in the country. After a more few miles, I began to get uneasy about our personal conversation, and then I really got nervous when he kept patting me on my leg and then later started to run his hand up and down my left leg. Then I really got shook up when he looked at me and said, "Do you like to play around with older men?"

I said "Hell no! Let me out right now!"

He just shut up and didn't say another word until we got to Waynesville, where I wasted no time in getting out of his car. *What a weirdo*, I thought, and to think he had such a pretty new black Ford sedan, the prettiest and only new car I had ever seen.

When I was fourteen, another monumental event occurred in my life. It was the day I got my first electric steel guitar. I had made up my mind for quite some time that I didn't want to spend my musical career beating rhythm and playing chords only for someone else to be the star. So one day while in the outhouse, I picked up the Montgomery Ward catalog and right there before my eyes in the music section was a beautiful solid-wood electric Hawaiian-style lap steel guitar on sale for only twenty-nine dollars.

I ordered it COD, and a few short days later I got a notice from Mr. Beach that I had received a big package. He told me I needed almost thirty-five dollars to pay for it before he could let me have it. Even though I made plenty of money playing with Little Henry and working at the dairy, I spent it as fast as I made it, and I did not have thirty-five dollars cash. Thankfully, Miss Lilla went into her grocery-store cashbox and loaned me the money to go to the post office and get my new steel guitar. I think she saw how excited I was, and I believe she was also excited.

Later that day I rushed over to the dairy, washed the bottles, and hurriedly bottled the milk as fast as possible. I couldn't wait to get back home and get with Little Henry and let him show me how to tune the new steel guitar and start trying to learn to play it. When I opened the big box, I discovered it even came with a solid steel bar and some finger picks, and some instructions on how to play it.

Little Henry quickly figured out how to tune it, and I took it from there, figuring out the notes and the positions and how to pluck each string as needed and how to hold the steel bar. Only a few weeks before, I had seen a young fellow just slightly older than me named Donnie Scott from Brunswick playing a similar steel guitar, and I quickly remembered some ideas from his playing and knew what I needed to do. I wanted to play lead steel guitar like the songs on the radio and country-music records we listened to and also wanted to back up Little Henry and anybody else when they were singing.

I didn't have an amplifier when I got my first steel guitar, so when I played it alone I could barely hear what I was doing. I realized the steel guitar was solid and not like the acoustic guitar I had been playing until that time. Again, as in the past, I felt if I could whistle a song through then I could play it, so I began whistling songs to make them familiar to me. Two of the very first songs I learned to play on the steel guitar were "The Great Speckled Bird" by Roy Acuff and "The Filipino Baby" by Cowboy Copas. When we would play out in public, I would plug into Little Henry's amplifier, but later I bought a small amp from a pawn shop in Brunswick for twenty-five dollars.

Little did I know that when I came to Jacksonville some years later, I would buy me a new beautiful seven-string Rickenbacker steel guitar and a big new amplifier. Today I still have that black-and-white Rickenbacker steel guitar with a few dings in it from many years of use and dodging beer bottles while playing in rowdy places. I treasure it very much because of its many memories of the days when I depended on it for a living, which included some good times and some bad times in my life.

As I look back on my earliest years in Waynesville, before I started working at the dairy and playing quite often, I had a lot of good friends. One in particular was Earl Thompson. Earl and I would go fishing in the ponds around Waynesville. We would pick wild blackberries, and one day we even made some blackberry wine and drank it. It made us both giddy.

Another time I stole a package of RailRoad chewing tobacco from the store, and we each chewed it. I didn't know I was not supposed to swallow it, so I did and it made me dog-sick. Earl and I once worked in the tobacco field following his uncle Ward Proctor with a mule as it pulled a sled through the fields, and people were suckering and later picking and curing tobacco. Earl also learned to play the guitar with me and Little Henry, and often he accompanied us at nearby juke joints, such as the Goose or Jack's Shack.

Another close friend I made back then was Jack King. Jack and I once stole some cucumbers and ate them, and one time we even stole a watermelon and attempted to eat it, although it was very hot from the sunshine. Jack often teased me with his stories about the difference between males and females.

I really enjoyed being free and out in the country during the formative years of childhood. I wondered then and I still do now how radically different my life would have been if just a few years earlier back in Brunswick, my aunt Polly and Mrs. Leggett had made the decision to send me off to an orphanage instead of moving Paul and I out to Brantley County. I doubt seriously that I would have turned out to be the same person I am today.

After completing the seventh grade in Waynesville, I went on to high school, riding the bus to Nahunta, eleven miles away. I attended that school from the eighth through the eleventh grades, graduating in 1947. In those days, rural high schools only gave eleven years of education.

When I was in the ninth grade, my daddy's work had ceased, and instead of looking for work elsewhere, he just came to live with us in Waynesville, knowing the ladies would take care of all of us. I soon realized that he definitely had a drinking problem. No matter where we were going together in his car, he'd always leave us in the backseat and go in and buy a bottle of liquor. Perhaps it was because of losing his wife while she was giving birth to my younger brother years earlier.

Dad drove an old rattletrap 1940 model Plymouth, which he allowed me to use on a few occasions. Because I worked at the dairy and played with Little Henry sometimes in the evenings, my father and I spent very little time together. Deep down, I may have harbored a resentment against him. I am sorry, but I have thought about that many times in years past.

I didn't do much dating in those years. I would often go to the high-school basketball games and to my friends' houses when they would have a party. Sometimes I was invited and sometimes I was not. I always had some kind of inferior feeling about myself because my home life was very much different from the other boys and girls. I had no parents in my upbringing, and my home life involved living in a house with Mrs. Leggett and two old maids.

When I was around other guys talking about their family life, I would shy away from them. I realized how drastically different my home life was from theirs when they talked about their mom and dad or brothers and sisters. I suppose that is one of the reasons I stayed on the job working at the dairy and spent much of my spare time playing one of my guitars. It was an escape for me from the real world.

I only had one high-school sweetheart, and she lived in a community about four miles away. She was a pretty girl, and I think she understood my background of working most of the time and playing when I could and that my home life was somewhat different from the others. Her name was Velma Jean Cox, and I dated her mostly through our senior year. Whenever I could get my daddy's old Plymouth, we would go to a movie, a peanut boiling, a party, or maybe a cane grinding or a basketball game. It could have been that Velma Jean was attracted to me because I had money in those days from working, and I probably spent a lot of it on her.

During the last three or four months of my high-school years, while we were on the school bus coming home one day, the school-bus driver suddenly had some kind of a seizure or fit. He began trembling and shaking all over and uttering strange words, with saliva or something running out of his mouth. He almost wrecked the bus and could have seriously hurt or even killed someone.

After some of the fellows and I got him subdued, there was no one nearby to call on for help—no traffic, no telephones. So I slid myself under the wheel and drove the bus on to Waynesville and then on to Browntown, taking all my friends home and leaving the bus and its keys for the school officials to find near Mr. McVeigh's store. I left the bus near the highway and went to do my late-afternoon chores of washing the bottles and bottling milk at the dairy.

When I got back, one of my buddies, L. D. Thompson, said, "Man, you are in deep shhhh ... *fertilizer.* The sheriff and the superintendent of schools have been down here looking for you, and they have been asking people all around here about what happened." L. D. even indicated they were going to lock me up.

I was scared half to death, but I stopped shaking long enough to go up to Mr. R. D. Driver, the superintendent of the Brantley Country School System, and face him. Gruffly he stated, "Rowland, you drove the school bus today, is that correct?"

I said, "Yes sir, we were stranded, and I was the only one on the bus that had a driver's license." I proudly I showed it to him.

He thought for a moment, and I'll never forget what he said next: "How would you like to drive it for the rest of the year?"

Needless to say, I was flabbergasted and somewhat thrilled at the idea. I would be making an additional $213 a month driving the bus for the coming three or four months, plus I would have all the gasoline my friends could syphon out of the tank, and Little Henry and I would have transportation to go out and play at various places at night. I must have been the richest, happiest young man in Waynesville, and maybe one of the more affluent in Brantley County at that time. By working at the dairy, playing with Little Henry, and now driving the school bus, I was making between $300 and $400 a month for the last few months of my high-school years. Today that would be the equivalent of a thousand or more dollars a month.

Where I spent it, I have no idea, but I always had two or three dollars in my pocket. I did not want to be caught dead broke. Many times I would spend my money by going to the drugstore in Nahunta not far from the high school for a good hot dog or something special like that for lunch. All I could think of in those days was getting out of school and being ready to face the world. Pete and Noody Gibson offered to send me to the University of Georgia upon my graduation, but I declined—much to my regret in later years.

After only ten years of schooling, I graduated from high school in May 1947. I knew that I didn't want to stay in Waynesville; I was ready to get out on my own. I quit the dairy and went to Brunswick looking for work, living with my older brother John and his wife, Francis, and their family. John had always kept an eye on his little brother even while we lived in Waynesville. He was very caring and special to me. He always welcomed me or any of our brothers in his home.

While living with John in Brunswick, I got a job at the Big Star Supermarket downtown, across from the Greyhound bus station—bagging groceries, stocking shelves, mopping the floor, and carrying out groceries for little old ladies. This job paid me twelve dollars a week, plus sometimes I'd make a dime carrying the groceries for the old ladies to their car. I hated that job and in general felt like I was just a flunky. It reminded me of how happy I was when I was back at the dairy doing what I really enjoyed. Back then I had friends, and I was being free.

After I had been at the supermarket for just over a month and had started playing on Saturday nights at the Goodyear Homes recreation center in Brunswick, I was making about twenty dollars a week total. I was still living with my brother John, but I did not like imposing on his family and I wanted to get out on my own. Every day when walking to work at the grocery store, I would pass a Plymouth and Dodge dealer that had a beautiful shiny new 1947 Plymouth convertible on the showroom floor, and I would stop and stare at how pretty it was, thinking to myself, *One day I'll have one of those.*

One Sunday I decided to go home for a visit to Waynesville and see my friends. My buddy L. D. told me that on the previous

Sunday, some big man and his wife who were driving a big Lincoln automobile with a bass fiddle on top were looking for me and had asked about me. At times during the previous year, I had heard Tiny Grier and the Florida Playboys on the radio on a station out of Jacksonville. Sometimes at home and even at school during lunch, we would listen to their live country-music radio show. They came on at twelve thirty every day.

I suppose the news that I could play a pretty good steel guitar had reached Jacksonville, and Mr. Grier wanted to get in touch with me. After visiting all my friends in Waynesville, I caught the bus back to Brunswick the next morning and went to work at the supermarket. For the first three or four days of that week, on the job mopping floors, all I could think of was Tiny Grier and playing in a band and being on the radio where all my friends could hear me. I hated the job of stocking shelves, toting groceries, or mopping the floors in a grocery store and being bossed around.

By Thursday of that week I had made up my mind to try to contact Mr. Grier. I went over to the Greyhound bus station next door on my lunch break and asked information to get me the radio station WJHP in Jacksonville, Florida, knowing that if they went on air at twelve thirty daily, they must be getting there earlier to rehearse. That call cost me seventy-five cents. Luckily I had three quarters in my pocket when I made the call to Mr. Grier.

After a few moments, Tiny Grier himself came to the phone. I told him who I was, and he sounded glad to hear from me. The band had hired a young black fellow named Ray Charles who was just out of the blind school in nearby St. Augustine. He had tried out and played with them for a few days and then abruptly left. About the same time he left, two others, PeeWee Jenkins and Cliff Austin, also left. He told me he needed musicians to keep his band going and the radio program alive and well.

I told him I was making twenty dollars a week and thought to myself, *If he pays me at least that much or maybe more than that, I'll leave and go to Florida.* I dang near dropped the telephone when he said they were averaging eighty to ninety dollars a week. Immediately I threw down my damned apron and told him I'd be there the following Sunday afternoon on the four o'clock bus. I wasn't going to let that opportunity pass.

I immediately went into the supermarket manager's office, handed him my apron, and told him I quit right then. In short, he could take this job and shove it! He looked me straight in the eye and said, "Don't ever use me for a recommendation for a job." To this day, I have never forgotten his words. I guess I should have given him more than fifteen minutes notice before leaving. I'll never do that again, but it was time for me to put my "fertilizer 'tween my toes" days behind me once and for all and head for the big city.

The very next day after I quit the supermarket, I went to Waynesville and got all my clothes and other belongings, including my steel guitar. I packed them in some paper bags I had quietly borrowed from the supermarket. Sunday morning, as I was leaving Waynesville to catch the bus, something happened I will never forget. My daddy, who was living with us at the time, walked with me to the bus stop. On the way, I noticed he had tears in his eyes.

My father was a very harsh man, and even though he had come to Waynesville to live with us two or three years earlier during my high-school years, he had never once shown either Bobby or me any love, caring, or emotional feelings. Never once had he said something like, "I'm proud of you" or "I love you boys." This would be the only time I can ever remember him showing any emotion for me or any of his sons.

I knew he loved me and I loved him, but neither of us would show it. I regret not having told him so that day. I thought surely there would be time for kind, loving words between us as I got older in life. I never dreamed I would never see him alive again— but that turned out to be true, because he died in the military hospital in Dublin, Georgia, just a few months later.

CHAPTER 2

COMING TO THE BIG CITY

On Sunday, July 6, 1947, when I got off the bus in Jacksonville about four o'clock in the evening, I had less than fifteen dollars in my pocket. Thankfully, Tiny Grier was there to meet me. We got in his big beautiful Lincoln and drove out toward the west side of Jacksonville where he lived.

As we were turning left off of Bay Street going west, I noticed a fellow standing by his car where his front wheel had simply wore out and fallen off on the ground, and he needed help. Tiny seemed to ignore him and just drove on by. That kind of stuck with me, because not stopping to help someone in need would never have happened back in Waynesville. *Oh well*, I thought. *That's the way it is here in the big city.*

The very next morning, on my first day with the Florida Playboys, I was sitting on the front porch of the boardinghouse on Edison Avenue where Tiny had made arrangements for me to live. The lady who ran the house was a Mrs. Beckner. She came outside and spoke to me very kindly as I was just sitting, staring at all the cars and trucks going up and down Edison Avenue. I had never seen so much traffic. After a brief chat about me and my past, she proceeded to go out into her front yard and do some yard work. Lo and behold, she fell tumbling down the stairs. I just sat there and stared down at her, and she looked up at me. My first thoughts were, *Well, I am now in the big city, and you just don't help people like her or anyone else in trouble in the big city. You mind your own business.* She must have thought I was a complete idiot.

The old lady didn't realize that at the age of sixteen and coming right out of the country, I had to learn the ways of the city people by not helping her up off the ground. I regretted that later on after I thought about it. Later, I apologized to her, and she laughed about my country ways. People do help people in the city just as we did back in the country. I am truly sorry for whatever thoughts she may have had about me, because I just didn't know better. After all, it was my first day in Jacksonville. Boy, was I naive, or just plain dumb. I thought about my days working at the dairy and how simple life had been just a few months ago. It made me wonder if I had done the right thing by leaving the simple life back up in South Georgia.

Every morning around ten o'clock, Tiny Grier would come by the boardinghouse and pick me up on his way to radio station WJHP, located in the *Jacksonville Journal* building in big beautiful downtown Jacksonville. We would usually get there an hour early to rehearse the songs we would sing and play that day. In a typical thirty-minute program, usually the leader Sleepy Gibbs would sing two or three songs and Marvin Phillips, Tiny Grier's son-in-law, would also sing two or three songs. The steel-guitar player and the fiddle player, Luther Moore, would each play one or two numbers to fill in our allotted time after the announcer Claude Taylor would do the commercial portion of the show. Our sponsors were Lynch/Davidson Ford Motors and Tillman's Laundry and Dry Cleaners.

After a few weeks of daily activity on the radio show, I began to get more confidence and took a larger part in our half-hour show. I began reading the fan mail that came in daily. I would occasionally tell a joke about our sponsors or listeners because I felt the band needed more than merely music to give it a lift and become more popular. You might say I became a practical joker while on the air as well as in our personal appearances.

One of our sponsors, Tillman's Laundry and Dry Cleaners, had printed up a gift certificate of one-dollar value, and from a distance it looked almost exactly like a dollar bill. Our trip daily from West Jacksonville to the radio station would take us directly into town on Beaver Street, which ran through a predominantly Negro area. There were always many black men standing around on the street corners, and as a joke at times, when Tiny would pull his big Lincoln up to a red light and just before driving off, I would take a Tillman's dollar, wad it up, and from the rear seat toss it out the window to a bunch of black men standing on the corner, yelling to them, "You all have a good time on us!" On one occasion, I looked through the back window and some of those guys almost got ran over by a car following us. They thought it was a real dollar bill. *Never again*, I thought, *but they did get a free laundry buck.*

My two and a half years of playing with the Florida Playboys were good. We had lots of fun and I met many people, and I learned the life of the big city. During that time, we had several memorable events. On one occasion, we played for a fundraiser at the George Washington Hotel. The main star was a young fellow flown in from Hollywood: Michael Landon. I met Michael because we were almost the same age, and he looked at me as if he knew me. I looked at him about the same way. Of course, I never saw him in person again after that.

On another occasion, the band was booked to play the Edison Pageant of Light in Fort Myers, Florida. It took us all day to drive down there, and then upon arriving, they put us up in a hotel, something I'd never stayed in before. Playing on the streets of Fort Myers for two nights before thousands of people was really a thrill.

One day, as we were preparing to go on the air, the great

Hank Williams and his Drifting Cowboys came into the station. Apparently they had agreed to appear in the Duval Armory with no prior promotion or advertising, and coming up and appearing on our program would help promote their attendance. During our half-hour show, Hank Williams did most of the talking and singing. He was tall and lanky fellow, and I wanted to play behind his singing, but it was not to be. He had his group with him. Before our thirty-minute show was over, the studio had become crowded with people from off the streets as well as the offices of the newspaper being published downstairs, all of them wanting to see or maybe meet the great Hank Williams.

A photographer came up from the *Jacksonville Journal* downstairs and took our picture. A picture of Hank Williams and his band along with Tiny Grier and the Florida Playboys is one of my most treasured items. After the show was over, I talked to his steel-guitar player, Don Helms, as well as his lead guitar player, Sammy Pruitt. I found out they were just good country musicians just as I was, but they had been lucky and they really enjoyed playing country music and traveling with Hank. They seemed to be good old down-to-earth people, and I was thrilled at the opportunity to meet them and Hank himself. He died a couple of years or so later, but I still treasure that picture to this day. I wanted to make sure it was in this book, because that was a momentous event in my life.

Hank Williams is on the far right and along the front row
are his band members Don Helms, Sammy Pruitt, and Jerry
Rivers. From left to right is our band leader Sleepy Gibbs,
(then, back row, left to right) Myself, then Moon Mullican a
recording artist, Tiny Grier, Lee Allen, and Marvin Phillips

Every day before our half hour on WJHP, the Mutual Broadcasting System had a fifteen-minute program for Purina Feeds featuring Eddie Arnold, the Tennessee Plowboy, with my steel-guitar idol, Little Roy Wiggins, and the rest of his band. This was a daily fifteen-minute show broadcast over five hundred stations nationwide. On one occasion, the Tennessee Plowboy came to WJHP and appeared with us on our program. I don't remember whether he sang a song or not, but I do remember him talking to our listeners and spending time with each of us after the show. He was alone and did not have his band.

Later I was taken by surprise when several people from all over Jacksonville told me that Eddie Arnold had played a song on his nationwide network program and dedicated it to the "old country boy" Marshall Rowland down in Jacksonville, Florida. Many years later, I had the opportunity to talk to Mr. Arnold at a CMA (Country Music Awards) convention in Nashville. He remembered me and dedicating that song to me. He ask me if I was still playing the steel guitar; I told him no, I had put it down, probably never to play it again. I now was into radio-station ownership, and that took my full time. I think he may have recognized my steel-guitar playing ability when he visited us years before, and just in case Little Roy Wiggins should leave him, he had someone else on tap.

One day just before we went on the air, three young fellows from Kissimmee, Florida, came into station WJHP. They were the Clements brothers: Gerald, Vassar, and Carroll. Tiny was rather reluctant to have them do a number for us, simply because he had not auditioned them before we went on the air. After talking to them and then after hearing them do only one song, we agreed all three were great musicians, and they did several songs featuring Vassar Clements on fiddle. He was great and would later go on to become one of Nashville's premier fiddle players. Vassar played on many recording sessions and on the Grand Ole Opry, as well as making personal appearances with many of the singing stars of Nashville.

On another occasion, a man who could pass as a hobo came to visit us at the radio station. His name was Irving Rouse, and he lived with his brother and his family near the railroad tracks in Miami, Florida. Tucked under his arm was the most raggedy old fiddle case I had ever seen. Irving and his brother, Gordon, had grown up playing the fiddle and guitar and had written a real fast fiddle tune called "The Orange Blossom Special." They had written other songs too, including one called "Mother's Not Dead, She's Only A-sleeping." Irving spent about two weeks every day on WJHP and traveled with us wherever we went to play dances.

During our intermissions or breaks, Irving would get out his violin and perform solo, entertaining the people by playing everything from classical music on down to hoedowns, including "The Orange Blossom Special." He would play that song and follow it with a down-home version of a Beethoven symphony. Irving would tell jokes, and on most nights he made more money than we did simply by passing the hat while entertaining the crowds when we were on a break. On one of our Thursday-night dances in Woodbine, Georgia, Mr. Rouse collected over a hundred dollars by wowing the folks.

He traveled with us every night in the Lincoln, and on one occasion he was sitting next to me in the backseat. I looked around and he had his pocketknife out and was scraping—yes, *scraping*—his teeth. He told me that was his way of cleaning his teeth. He needed a haircut badly, but he was indeed a great violinist. He played with us at all our dances, in Woodbine and Folkston, Georgia, at the Mandarin Athletic Club, St. Joseph's Parish Hall in South Jacksonville, and at St. Ambrose Parish Hall in Moccasin Branch, near Palatka. I was sorry the day he told us it was time for him to move on. I never saw him again after that.

While I was playing with the Florida Playboys, sometime in 1947 or early '48, WMBR radio was building the first television station to serve our area. Jacksonville had reached the pinnacle of having its very own TV station. Until that time, television was only available in the larger cities across America, most of them up north. The whole town was abuzz about the coming of this new form of "radio with pictures."

Channel 4 was built and went on the air before the coaxial cable arrived to bring network programming to the area. In the beginning, all of the new WMBR television programming had to originate locally. How it happened, I'm not sure, but the Florida Playboys were given a thirty-minute show each evening at five for several weeks. Since I had become thoroughly entrenched as the clown on our radio programs, I carried that same enthusiasm over to TV. I would read the fan mail, make jokes about the people who watched us, and so on. I had no fear of people who could now watch us perform instead of just listening to our band.

After that short stint on television, I was never as enchanted by TV as many radio announcers or personalities seem to have been. On a few occasions, I did do some work with channel 7, our community TV station. But they would only call when they held a country-music fundraiser-type show and I was invited to participate.

In November 1959, after two and a half years, my career with Tiny Grier and the Florida Playboys came to an abrupt end, on a sad note I will regret for the rest of my life. One night we had played at the officers' club at the naval air station. There was a big crowd of people, and they were all drinking, dancing, and having a good time, as many people did after the war was over. Usually when we played for a dance like this, we would take a break sometimes every hour or definitely every two hours. Our breaks would last about ten or fifteen minutes. That night was no different. It was a gala affair to say the least.

On the way home after the dance, Marvin, Sleepy, and I were in the backseat of the Lincoln. I casually told Sleepy about one or two of the people there coming up to me and complaining about him mooching drinks from them or from their table that night. The men told me they didn't like it. I said, "Sleepy, you should't do that," because it was getting to be a habit every time we played at a dance where there was drinking.

All he said was, "You don't know these people. They are my friends, and they like for me to drink with them."

I said, "That's not what the men told me, Sleepy. You got it all wrong. They were mad about you mooching their drinks that they had to pay for."

Sleepy again said, "You smartass, you don't know these people. I do, and they're my friends."

Over and over I explained to him that it wasn't the first time it had happened. It had happened several times in the weeks before. This type of conversation went on for probably five or ten minutes as he continued to call me a liar. Suddenly I exploded inside. I could take no more of it. I turned and hit him right in the middle of his face as hard as I could with my fist again and again. I was literally beating the daylights out of him because he had made me so mad by calling me a liar over and over and over.

Tiny stopped the car and pulled me off of Sleepy, and then he put me in the front seat with him and his wife while I calmed down. I quit the band that night when I got out of the car, and the next morning I packed up my clothes, took my guitar, and went back to Waynesville. I never played with them again. Sometime later, the band broke up and Tiny quit the music business. They had lost all their sponsors on their radio program.

After a couple of weeks back in Waynesville, however, I knew that I did not want to stay there. I had grown up there and still had friends there, but it was time for me to move on in life. My dad had passed away earlier that year, my brother Bobby had gone to Brunswick to live with my older brother John, and my other brother Paul was off still in the Navy. I took the almost $400 I had saved up and gave all but $50 of it to the old ladies in the store and to Mrs. Leggett, who had taken care of me. I left and went back to Jacksonville to my old boardinghouse, even though I had very little money. For some reason, I did not panic. It cost me very little to live at that time, only fifteen dollars a week for the boardinghouse and a little money for gas for my 1946 Ford.

I started hanging around the radio station WJHP, where I already knew most of the employees. Two of them would become my good friends and later were to be my mentors: Claude Taylor and Chaz Harris. I would run and get them coffee, pull records for them, and refile the records later. I would have probably swept the building if they had asked me to. In short, I had nothing else to do and nowhere to go to spend my time.

CHAPTER 3

MY NEW CAREER AS A RISING STAR

At WJHP, I had started opening the new records that came in and putting them away in proper order so they could be found and played as needed. This was a job no one else seemed to want, especially the DJs. At that time, the station had what is known as *block programming*, meaning a half hour of this or another hour of that. From nine-thirty to ten each morning, a fellow named Smiley Smith had a country-music show on the station playing records and also strumming his guitar as he talked. He had a couple of sponsors, but he had abruptly quit and gone to a new station in town.

As fate would have it, the following week I opened a new Columbia record and found something by a fellow named Little Jimmy Dickens titled, "I'm Just a Plain Old Country Boy." Bingo—a light turned on in my head. Since playing in the band had taught me not to fear radio, I took the record in to the manager and told him if he'd let me have Smiley's half hour, I would play this record as my theme song and try to get some more advertisers. He agreed and said, "Let's try it for a few weeks."

The rest is history. I was off and running with a chance for a new career. Little did I know it was to be the beginning of my life in radio.

Trying to look smart for my first radio job

I contacted all the advertisers I had ever met or known of while playing with the Florida Playboys and asked them to try advertising with me. For insurance, I told them if they bought a one-minute spot for three dollars, I would give him two or three minutes or whatever it took to get people into their store. It worked, and among my first advertisers were Paschal Brothers Hardware, Ralph Little Jewelers, Mcduff Appliances, and Rockwood Hardware—and so many more that one day the manager suggested I take the entire hour from nine until ten each morning. I did. That hour was following a real gentleman who was a long time institution in Jacksonville for many years, Mr. Lazybones, Ted Chapeau.

A few weeks later, while I was on the air one morning, I received a call from Mr. Hoyt Cotney, who had been listening to me and liked what he heard. Mr. Cotney owned and operated one of the biggest tire companies in Jacksonville. He told me that he would buy a full half hour of my show for $500 per month, but it had to be between six and seven in the morning when people were going to work, especially in the rural areas around Jacksonville. I took his message and his offer to the manager, Mr. Milford Reynolds, and he approved it. In fact, he suggested I take the two full hours from six to seven and from nine to ten.

That only lasted two weeks. Mr. Chapeau apparently didn't like being sandwiched in between two hour-long south-Georgia-style country-music shows. He left the station and went back to his original station, WMBR 1460.

Now I really was in hog heaven, because the manager gave me the entire four-hour segment from six to ten, six days a week, on a 5,000-watt 1320 AM radio station owned by the *Jacksonville Journal*. The evening newspaper constantly promoted my show along with other programs on the radio station on one of two major Jacksonville newspapers. They even took a picture of me out at a mule farm, holding a phonograph record up high.

I got a thrill during the first couple of months of on-the-air mornings when I received a letter from a Mr. Halle Cohen, owner of Cohen Brothers, the largest department store in Jacksonville, located downtown right next door to the *Journal* building. He told me to keep up the good work but asked me to play more songs from a newcomer named George Jones. I was honored to get a letter from a man of his stature, and needless to say, I fulfilled his request.

Also at that time, I had formed a small band of my own with two or three fellows, and we began playing for dances on Saturday nights at the Mandarin Athletic Club. Along with other chatter each morning, I most certainly promoted our dances. I suppose my country humor and wit were intriguing to the city folks who never knew our kind of lifestyle.

One morning around six thirty, I received a phone call from a man identifying himself as Jim Reeves. It seems he and his band had been passing through town when his bus had a flat tire, and while getting it repaired they were eating breakfast, and that's when he decided to call me. *What a thrill*, I thought. He and I talked on the air for about fifteen minutes about his RCA Victor records and his appearing on the Grand Ole Opry, and also about the fact that he was an airplane pilot, which I had at one time wanted to be.

That was one interview I never forgot, and I wish I had recorded it. He died some years later in bad weather in a crash with his airplane. Jim Reeves had some great records in his career, "Four Walls" and "He'll Have to Go." I was very saddened to hear of his passing, because just from that fifteen-minute interview, I could tell he was a good, genuine person. I guess that was why he got the title "Gentleman" Jim Reeves.

At one point, WJHP hired a program director from Waycross, Georgia, by the name of Ron Tuten, and he wanted to do a Saturday-night hit parade from eight till midnight. He suggested that I do a one-hour Saturday-night barn dance from seven until eight. I only did the program for a few months, because my advertisers just weren't interested.

However, one night about seven forty-five, while I was on the air, a young fellow walked into the station wearing white buck shoes. It turned out to be Pat Boone. He had cut his first records and was in town visiting his grandparents, and he was visiting the station to get his records played. I heard later he was born in Jacksonville. For about fifteen minutes, Ron Tuten and I talked to him and about his career. I wasn't sure at that time whether his recordings were going to go country or pop, but as it turned out, both kinds of stations programmed him, and he was all the better for it. He later married the daughter of Red Foley, one of our best early country music stars.

Pat is indeed a great guy and a true Christian. At the time of our meeting, I thought him to be a couple of years younger than me, but he was really enthusiastic about his music. I learned a lot about Nashville and the recording industry from his visit that

night, because it was all new to me at that time. At one time in my
early years, I thought deeply about moving to Nashville. I guess it
was because of my love for country music.

I must admit that during those five or six years that I was
on the air as a young whippersnapper disc jockey on WJHP, not
everything went the way I wanted. In fact, sometimes things
appeared to be disastrous.

One morning a policeman called me from the Liberty Street
police headquarters and asked me to play a song for a buddy
of his, a well-known fellow policeman whose name I will not
mention. I'll call him Officer B. He was a ruddy red-faced gent
who, according to his fellow policemen, was known to imbibe on
occasion, even sometimes while on the job, whereby they would
poke fun at his drinking habits. The policeman told me to play
him a drinking song and tell him to wake up and get on the ball
over there at the police substation on the south side.

Since it was a policeman who had called me, I certainly didn't
doubt his honesty or his words, and I most certainly wanted to
fulfill his wish. I dug up a record by Red Foley called "I Got
Drunk Again," and I played it for Officer B. at the south-side
substation, making a smart remark about his past. I should not
have done that. Apparently, he didn't like it, and in a few days the
radio station received a letter from his lawyer saying he was suing
for damage to his character and putting his job in jeopardy. They
never told me how it was settled, but I assume the station paid
Mr. B. and his attorney.

I learned a lesson the hard way about making a smart remark
about someone's reputation. I felt it almost cost me my job, just
doing something stupid trying to please a police officer I respected
while he was making a joke at a fellow cop.

Another day after I got off the air on WJHP, the manager,
Mr. Reynolds, called me into his office and closed the door.
Immediately I knew something was wrong. He showed me three
letters he had received in the mail requesting, or rather *demanding*,

that I be taken off the air. I assumed it was just some irritated egghead listener who was disgruntled, and I passed it off and soon forgot about it.

Ten days later, Mr. Reynolds called me into his office again. He had received perhaps a dozen more letters asking that the illiterate trash in the mornings on one of Jacksonville's major radio facilities be removed. All of the handwritten letters were different and stated that the fellow doing the program was an illiterate hillbilly who was polluting young children's minds with his corny, sometimes off-color humor and lowdown style of country music.

The more I read the dozen or so letters, the more I got all shook up. I told Mr. Reynolds that if he thought it best, I would quit WJHP and my career. He assured me that someone or something was behind all of this.

As luck would have it, several months later I started dating a pretty young blonde girl named Pat Fowler. Pat told me one night while we were on a date about an assignment one of her college girlfriends had been given by a professor or teacher at Jacksonville University. The students were to write letters to station WJHP and its management, describing me as trash and my humor as more trash and stating that all that on-air pollution was not in the best interests of the people in our community—it was demeaning to the citizens of Jacksonville. Pat's friend had been told by the teacher that the student with the best letter damning my show would get the highest grade.

I could not believe anyone at a great private university like Jacksonville University, would think of such an idiotic assignment. But deep down, I really felt relieved after that discovery was made. I felt sorry for the man or woman, whether a professor or just a teacher, who would have such harsh feelings against country music and my "Old Country Boy" morning show as to instigate such an assignment to their students. He or she needed to get some good old fertilizer 'tween their toes and grow up.

I had some good times during my five-and-a-half-year stint at

WJHP. My brother Bobby had graduated from Glynn Academy in Brunswick and had come down to live with me. He worked at the Great Southern Trucking Company and made a lot of friends there. He was making good money and had his own automobile. In fact, he paid half the rent when we lived in a boardinghouse together on Oak Street in Riverside.

At the radio station, I was making fifty dollars a week guaranteed and 15 percent of all my advertising sales. Sales were over $4,000, so I earned about $1,000 most months. That was good money for me, and I was very happy to get it—plus my little band and I played weekly at the Mandarin Athletic Club.

I got a call one day from a gentleman named Harold Cohn who said he was building a new radio station in Jacksonville and would like to have me do my morning show. He suggested I meet him in his office. Reluctantly, I met with him. But I was happy where I was at WJHP and I told him so. He inquired about my business and said I would fit right in with his plans to build an all-country music station on 1400kc. He already had plans for Frank Thies, his engineer, to take over four hours in the late evening, and another fellow named Randy Jones would program country music during the day. Randy Jones was also known as Uncle Jess.

After I told Mr. Cohn how much advertising I was grossing, he said, "Come over to my station and I'll give you 50 percent of your gross advertising dollars." *Wow*, I thought, as I nearly fell out of my chair talking to him. That was almost twice as much as I was currently making. I had to think about it, so I told him I would call him back in a few days.

A couple of days went by and his offer weighed heavily on me, so I decided the best thing to do to give me peace of mind was to go in and talk to Mr. Reynolds about Mr. Cohn's offer. Without hesitation, Mr. Reynolds said, "We'll match it!" I couldn't believe it. Without any effort at all or even asking for it, I had almost doubled my income.

I was ready to go somewhere and celebrate, maybe even start

drinking, which I had never done. I determined later the reason he did that was John H. Perry, one of the wealthiest men in Florida and the owner of the *Jacksonville Journal* and WJHP radio had plans to build a second television station in Jacksonville. It would be on channel 36, and at the same time he had a permit to build channel 2 in Daytona Beach. Meanwhile, Mr. Reynolds was told not to "shake the boat," because Perry had bigger and better plans for Jacksonville.

On several occasions while I was on the air at WJHP, the salespeople excitedly told me about a thing call a Hooper rating, a survey that was taken every six months to show all the local radio stations' standings in listenership. On one occasion, the ratings had just come out, and the sales guys pointed out to me that for the six months preceding, my morning show had placed number one in audience in Jacksonville between eight and nine in the morning, and for the rest of that period never below third place.

Boy was I proud. On occasion, I still wondered about the days just few short years prior when I was working at the dairy. But now I was riding high. I had bought myself a new yellow Chevrolet convertible, and truly I thought of myself as being a "man about town."

At one time while I was a disc jockey on the *Journal* station, I became very good friends with my afternoon competitor, Frank Thies. About a year later, I bought a boat from him. My brother Bobby and I really enjoyed being out with that boat almost every weekend. We were constantly out on the water with it somewhere around the Jacksonville area, and one of our favorite spots was Cedar Creek. There were always plenty of good-looking girls and guys out for the weekend—some fishing, some dancing at a nearby restaurant and even drinking there, others just wanting to get out of the house.

I will never forget one day when Bobby and I were cruising up and down the creek, and a gentleman standing on the shore waved to me to come over. It seems he had been bragging to his six or eight friends with him that he could waterski on one ski and never get wet. He asked if I would pull him fast so he could show off in front of his friends. He must have thought I was a pro at running a boat and pulling skiers.

Nothing could have been farther from the truth. But being proud of my new boat and its power, I immediately agreed. He took his shoes and socks off and rolled up his britches and stood in the water about twelve or fourteen inches deep. He told me that when he waved to me, I should hit full throttle, whereby he would come up and out of the water with only one ski.

It was amazing, I had never done that before. I must've pulled him around ten or fifteen minutes or more, because he was doing all kind of fancy maneuvers on that one ski and never getting his clothes wet. After a few moments, he waved me to drop him off at the shore where his friends were still standing and watching his performance. I merely throttled back and pulled the boat straight up to the shore and eased up on the sandbar. I had stopped, but little did I realize he was still out in the water the length of the ski rope in the middle of the creek about ten feet deep. I looked back and saw him bobbling up and down with all his clothes, his watch and his billfold still in his pocket.

I should have asked him how to stop and tow or sling him up near the shore where he could off without getting wet. But I was so excited, I never though to. Instead, Bobby threw his danged ski rope to him and I took off. I remember looking back, and he was still shaking his fist at me while trying to stay afloat and make it to shore.

As I mentioned earlier, when I first went on the air at WJHP, I organized a small band. After all, I had been playing since I was twelve years old, and playing the steel guitar since I was fourteen. I suppose I was pretty well-known in the area as a country musician. My band onsisted of a rhythm-guitar player named Bill

Yeomans and a young drummer named Johnny Blackshear. Over time, we had different lead guitar or fiddle players that made up our band.

Our big event would be Saturday nights at the Mandarin Athletic Club, where we had built up a huge following over the months and years we played there on Saturday nights. We had very few fights or other trouble. Bobby would handle the ticket sales and the money, and the band and I would entertain the people by playing for their dancing or listening pleasure.

Since I promoted our appearances on my morning show, people came from all over Jacksonville and would always seem to have a good time. On a few occasions, some navy guys from Mayport would have a little too much to drink and cause trouble, but we always had county police on hand to keep order. We split up the money we took in each Saturday night in the following manner: I took one third, while Bobby and the musicians and the policeman on duty would split the other two-thirds. I hardly ever made less than a hundred dollars a night. At one New Year's Eve dance, we took in over a thousand dollars at the door.

I had one of the most memorable days in my life while I was a disc jockey on WJHP. It happened in late 1950 or maybe early 1951. I was contacted by the office of Colonel Tom Parker by his right-hand fellow, whose name was Bevo. The meeting was regarding Colonel Tom bringing the largest country music show ever in our area to the Jacksonville Gator Bowl. Among the lineup of country-music stars he had signed up were Hank Snow, Faron Young, Ferlin Husky, Patsy Cline, Hawkshaw Hawkins, the Wilburn Brothers and, for variety, two newcomers to the music and entertainment scene: "Deacon" Andy Griffith and a young upstart named Elvis Presley.

Elvis was just beginning to wow audiences everywhere with his hip-swinging rockabilly sound, and that was just what I always played for my lively morning show. He was then recording for Sun

Records. Andy Griffith had recorded a monologue on Capitol records called "What It Was, Was Football." I tried to keep my morning show upbeat, and I played and laughed at his talking records many times on my morning show. From the phone calls that came in to me daily, my listeners liked Andy Griffith too.

At a meeting approximately a month before the show was scheduled for the Gator Bowl, we met with Colonel Tom Parker himself. There were four of us involved: Mae Axton, Glenn Reeves, Frank Thies and myself. After he laid out all his plans for the show, his words to us were, "Don't worry. Work hard and promote this great concert, the first and largest ever to come to Jacksonville, and the colonel will take care of you."

**Glen Reeves, Mae Axton, Me and Frank all discussing
Colonel Tom's country music extravaganza**

Frank Thies was then on WRHC 1400kc playing country music, and Glenn Reeves was on WPDQ 600kc. I suppose Mae

Axton was the coordinator. I was really excited about being able to promote this big show on my morning radio program. I am certain I promoted it far more than either Frank or Glenn, because station management didn't seem to care as long as I brought in the money from my advertisers.

As the week of the big event approached, I started plugging it almost between every record on my morning show, going on about how great the show was going to be and how fortunate Jacksonville was to have such a gigantic lineup at one time. Two days before the show, I got so excited, I rented a pair of loudspeakers and put them on top of my car and rode all over Jacksonville ballyhooing the big show. It almost sent me to jail.

I pulled up at a red light out in the northwest section of Jacksonville on Eighth Street and turned the volume up real loud, blasting away the big news about the show coming to town this Saturday night. Moments later, a motorcycle cop with red lights flashing pulled me over. As he got out his ticket book he said, "What do you think you're doing?"

I told him who I was and that I was ballyhooing the big show coming to the Gator bowl on Saturday night. He sternly replied, "No you are not—not in this spot. Move on or go to jail."

I suddenly realized I was only a couple hundred feet outside St. Luke's Hospital. He let me go, reminding me that there were sick people in there and they did not want me with my loudspeakers to wake them up—or even worse, shake up a doctor who might be in the middle of a heart operation or something worse. He said to me, "Move on, Old Country Boy!" and I did. Thank you, sir! My morning radio show had saved me a ticket or possible incarceration.

WJHP radio was owned by the *Jacksonville Journal*, and at that time the owner, Mr. John H. Perry, also owned a second TV station on the air in Jacksonville. I don't think the station had many viewers, because it was on channel 36 and in order to receive it, each TV set had to have a little box or converter sitting on top or nearby. It had been on the air for several months and was located out on Philips Highway in an old nightclub called the Peacock Club, which had closed down.

About a week prior to the show at the Gator Bowl, Tom Gilchrist, then manager of the radio station, came to me and asked how I'd like to have all the stars out for a two-hour live television interview on the day of the show. I was excited about the opportunity to meet and see in person all my country-music favorites and be with them for this television event. I immediately contacted Colonel Tom Parker's office, and they assured me they would arrange to have most of the stars on hand for what was going to be a big TV interview.

At the interview, Ferlin Husky, Hank Snow, one of the Wilburn brothers, Andy Griffith, and Elvis Presley all showed up. We had a good two-hour session sitting around talking about their past and their rise to stardom. Andy Griffith was a professor or a teacher somewhere in North Carolina when he cut his "Football" record. All in all, I thought it went very well, because I got all of them to speak up about their past and mostly about their country-music careers.

After the TV interview, Elvis wanted to go downtown and buy some shoes and maybe some clothes. The rest of the fellows rode back to the Roosevelt Hotel in their taxi, and I spent three or four hours privately with Elvis. At the time, he was about seventeen years old and I was just two years older, so we had a lot in common. Apparently neither of us had a steady girl, so we really got into some personal discussions (some I can't put in this book) about women.

Since Elvis had been garnering quite a lot of attention in those early years, particularly in the South, he constantly talked about the girls in other cities and wanted to compare them with young women or girls in Jacksonville and elsewhere in Florida. Were they pretty? Did they really wear bikinis on the beach or maybe sometimes go naked? But most of all, would they put out?

We jokingly chatted about how our lives were similar, with our musical backgrounds and how we both had been bitten by the show-business bug and wound up where we were that day, him with his recent Sun recordings being played nationwide and me with my daily top-rated local country-music show.

I drove all the way back to town and parked my car, and the two of us wandered up Adams Street. I took him to Rosenblooms and Furchgotts clothing store. He and I wandered through the store, but I don't remember whether he bought anything. At one point in our stroll, he stopped and said something to a pretty young girl inside the ticket booth outside the old Palace theater. I couldn't hear what he said, but I remember the young lady blushed red.

Elvis was a virile young man, much as I was back then, and while I can't remember everything we talked about, I do remember that most of our conversation centered around girls as opposed to his music or his future. He did ask if I was playing his records, and indeed I was. I liked to keep my morning show upbeat, and almost all his first Sun recordings were fast-paced. From those chats, it's clear that neither I nor Elvis, in either of our wildest of dreams, would have believed that he would someday become the King, idolized by the millions of fans worldwide that he would gather over his lifetime.

That night, over thirty thousand people turned out for the show at the Gator Bowl. Colonel Tom told us to come up to his hotel room in the Roosevelt Hotel, and he would pay us for our efforts. I was holding my breath because of all the hard work I had done, and all I had was his words, "the colonel will take care of you." I knew I had done much more to promote that show than all the others combined. In the last two weeks, almost every record I played was by one of the stars on the show, and I talked about the show between every record. I was holding my breath at how much we were going to make.

When we got to his room, Colonel Tom put a rubber band around four rolls of big bills and without hesitation threw them all down on the floor. Within three seconds, I hit the floor—before Frank, Glenn, or Mae Axton even knew what was taking place. I wanted to make dang sure I got one of those big rolls of bills. We were each paid whopping $1,000 for our work. I firmly believe it was at this event that Colonel Tom or someone from his office must have listened to a new song Mae Axton had cowritten with a steel-guitar player named Tommy Durden. The name of the song was "Heartbreak Hotel," and we all know it sold millions of records for Elvis.

Elvis would later play the Florida Theatre in downtown Jacksonville and was reprimanded somewhat by a local judge who didn't seem to like his hip-swinging antics. At that time, my wife and I were in Fernandina Beach running our first radio station, and we decided not to go and see Elvis perform.

Many years later, when WQIK was nearing its peak, I was contacted by Colonel Tom and told he wanted to bring Elvis to Jacksonville. I called and got the dates and all the info necessary and went to work clearing two dates for Elvis—a Friday night in Macon and the following Saturday night in Jacksonville. The coliseum managers jumped at the idea and began shuffling already booked events around in order to clear the dates Colonel Tom wanted. Some events booked well in advance had to be cancelled, but the venue managers knew how big this show would be.

After two weeks on the long-distance phone, which cost me a lot in those days, we had it all set. I immediately called the colonel and excitedly told him it was all set. He said, "Great, now send me a binding cashier check for $150,000 and it's a done deal!" Needless to say, I dang near fell out of my chair. I could probably have borrowed it, but I sure didn't have it in my back pocket. And even if I had it, I would not have gambled up front for a live show with it—too many things can happen before the show date. Elvis did come to Macon and Jacksonville, and Colonel Tom spent a measly $500 with our station for advertising. My wife and I went to see Elvis at that show, and he appeared to be grossly overweight at that time—certainly no longer the young man I had once spent the evening with.

I'll never forget the day Elvis died. My family and I, along with my son's girlfriend, Michelle, had just arrived back in the USA after two weeks in the Bahamas crammed together on my boat. Brian and Michelle got off the boat at Francis Langford's marina in Stuart and went to the nearest 7-Eleven store for refreshments. Minutes later, they came running back to the boat, yelling that Elvis has died. We were all very saddened to hear about it.

Marshall Rowland's philosophy on the radio industry is simple: Stay away from overly-competitive big-city markets, get the whole family involved . . . and never retire!

Back to work at the office

Without a doubt, the most wonderful thing that ever happened to me happened in June 1953, while I was at the peak of my WJHP career. That's when a young lady named Carol Casey applied for a job at the station. While she was waiting to be interviewed, she saw me through the glass studio window filing records away from my morning show. She asked the receptionist, "Who is that man?"

Our cute receptionist, Betty Langdon, replied, "Why, that's Marshall Rowland, our number-one star personality here."

I do believe from that moment on that Carol had her eye on me, and I know I had my eye on her. She was right out of college and was hired immediately by the station as a copywriter and traffic director, scheduling our commercials. I was smitten from that day on.

I started seeing Carol almost every day for lunch and in the evenings after work. After all, she only made thirty-five dollars a week, which was hardly enough to get by on. Plus she needed a proper introduction to the big city by a big-shot like me, since she was from the little town of St. Marys. I took her to lunch almost every day and out to dine at night. It was only a short time later that I would ask her to marry me.

Being rather old-fashioned, she insisted we talk to her parents first before she gave me her yes. The very next Sunday, we drove down to Clearwater Beach, Florida, where her parents were vacationing to ask for their permission to get married. Her daddy, Edison Casey, immediately said yes, but her mother was rather hesitant. In fact, it looked like she would almost faint before she finally gave her permission. I suppose as a mother, she wanted the very best for her only daughter, and marrying a roustabout country boy from Waynesville was not what she had in mind.

Unbeknownst to me, I had a history with Carol and her family that started long before we actually met. As my mother-in-law tells it, during the time when I was playing with the Florida Playboys, Carol came home on vacation from Wesleyan College one weekend. Since they were considered affluent, they were probably one of the few families in St. Marys to own a TV set.

Carol's mother had become a television junkie and must have watched everything channel 4 put on the air. On that trip home from college, she yelled to Carol, "Come here! I want you to see this nut on television!" That was me, and she could have hardly imagined then that her daughter would be that nut's loving wife for more than fifty-seven years.

We were married May 16, 1954, in the Methodist church where Carol grew up. Her daddy was in the shrimp and timber business, and even had the church painted just for our wedding. As the day of our wedding approached, I got more and more apprehensive—or just downright scared about my future. I had heart pangs about losing my position as what I thought was one of Jacksonville's most eligible young men and losing all the money I was making from WJHP and playing dances. But I knew deep down I was ready for marriage. I was tired of chasing girls and catering to them, especially when they would call in on my radio show.

On the day we were married, all three of my brothers were my best men: Bobby, Paul and John. The church was full of flowers and people. The preacher who officiated suggested that Bobby and I wait outside in back of the church and enter on signal at an appointed time. I can honestly tell you I thought about running off through the nearby woods at the last moment and getting out of this noose that was about to be placed around my neck, perhaps forever. My life as a young roustabout was coming to an end.

Thankfully, though, I did not run at that moment but wound up marrying what I thought was the most wonderful girl in the world. We went on our honeymoon to New Orleans, and those first days of our marriage were full of happy memories. Just to prove it, our son Marshall Jr., or Marty, was born nine months and eleven days after that wedding.

Within the first year of our marriage, Carol insisted that I join the church we were attending at the time, Lakewood Methodist.

I did and was baptized by Rev. John White, who at that time was hardly any older than I. Indeed, that too was a day I will never forget.

While we both worked at WJHP, I continued to play at dances from time to time, saving my money because Carol and I both knew we wanted our own radio station. Together we had saved over $8,000. I felt that between the two of us, we would be successful at whatever we did in radio in the future.

My first thoughts were to start looking out of town for a city near Jacksonville that had no radio station, because a license from the FCC would be easier to obtain. I first looked at Starke, Florida, and while on one of my visits there, I met the supervisor for Setzer's Supermarkets. He suggested I look at Fernandina Beach, because their store in Fernandina did much more business than the Starke supermarket. He had heard me on the radio many times in the past and seemed eager to help me. I will never forget Willie Wates for his guidance. He told me because of the pulp mills in Fernandina Beach, the economy was much better. People had more money to spend.

He was right! Not only was the economy better, but Carol had relatives in Fernandina Beach, and the city of St. Marys where she was from was only six air miles away across the marsh. It was like a light had turned on in my head. In the months after Carol and I married, I began to feel more and more confident that the two us could own and operate our very own station. With her handling the inside office work and me on the air and out selling advertising during the day, I just had a good feeling that we could make it on our own. So with that kind of confidence, we planned our first radio station.

The consultant who would help me build the station and file the necessary FCC papers was a gentleman from Palatka, Florida, named Mac McCall. We originally filed for 800kc, but later the FCC told us to amend our application to 1570kc. We went on the air on Labor Day 1955 with WFBF in Fernandina Beach, Florida.

The day we went on the air, I had no money for our first payroll. So I borrowed $2,000 to cover our first few weeks on the air. The two years we spent in Fernandina Beach were perhaps our happiest, because we met people who were like us, young couples just starting out in married life. We were invited to dances, and we participated in practically all the city events. I joined the Lions Club, and even before the station was built, when we were yet to receive our permit from the FCC, Carol and I along with our newborn son, Marty, moved into our first home, a small house on the outskirts of Fernandina Beach. We immediately began to be active in the Memorial Methodist Church, and more and more we came to know the leading citizens of the community.

After we were on the air just a few weeks, one evening the area had a bad thunderstorm that knocked out the electricity to the downtown area. Our minister, Rev. Bill Boland, lived near that area, and each morning he would take a stroll down Atlantic Avenue and on many mornings visit with me at the studios of WFBF. This particular morning, I noticed that my clock on the wall was off time because of the previous evening's storm, so when Rev. Boland came strolling in, I asked him to tell me the correct time so I could set my clock. Darned if he didn't preach an entire sermon the following Sunday on "Things aren't always what they appear to be—recently the local radio station asked *me* for the correct time, when every day I had been setting my watch by their time."

At the time we went on the air in Fernandina Beach, we only had one child, our oldest son, Marty. One day, Carol had taken Marty in his crib to work with her while she prepared the program log, wrote the necessary copy for commercials, and did an air show from ten until twelve noon. A well-dressed gentleman named Howard Connors from New York City once stopped by our offices to sign us up for ASCAP music. The man from ASCAP had apparently visited hundreds of radio stations in his travels all over the USA, but he went out to his car, got his camera, came back in, and took pictures of my wife and son. He said he was going back to New York and taking this memorable visit with him, as he had never been in a radio station with a young baby in a crib nearby.

I have always had an affinity for airplanes. As a kid, I would whittle the warplanes I heard about from any old piece of wood. I was approached by a group of Fernandina Beach businessmen to invest with them and buy an airplane. *Wow*, I thought, *something I've always wanted to do is learn to fly*. I invested $100 along with six others, and we bought an old Taylorcraft for just $700. How old it was, I didn't care to know. It had no radio, no electronics, only an altimeter. One of the investors was an instructor who taught me to fly, and I soloed after only twelve hours of tutoring.

The very next day after I soloed, I went out to the airport, climbed in the old T-craft, and took off. After a half hour or so, I flew over to Cumberland Island. *How beautiful*, I thought as I looked down from the air. Disregarding my teacher's advice from the day before to let him check me out before I tried to land anywhere except the airport, I decided to land on the beach.

That morning there was an abnormally high tide that had washed the pristine white sands and left them wet. From the air, it looked to be hard-packed. When my wheels touched the ground, however, the plane kept trying to flip over. After three times of the tail almost hitting the sky (I thought), I gave it full throttle, only to hit a soft spot and spin around on the beach. How close I came to death I really don't know, but I sure did thank the Lord for saving me. When I got home, I got some clean underwear.

I had sold out the entire radio station with commercials at "a dollar a holler." One of our better promotions during our first days in Fernandina Beach was a contest whereby a listener would write in and give us a name of what WFBF meant. A local listener won with this: "WFBF means We Feed Bull Frogs." That listener must have known that we had placed our antenna right in the middle of a marshy, swampy area. He won a free meal at the 5 J's Restaurant.

During the two years in Fernandina Beach, we programmed anything we could sell advertising on. For instance, we would go out and tape-record baseball or football games and air them later with a sponsor. We had a local fellow who worked for Rayonier come in each evening and do a fifteen-minute sports show. We tried to cover all the local happenings and make big news items out of them.

My engineer/announcer was George Duck from Palatka, and not only did he build the station from the ground up, but he was very helpful in our small-town programming, especially the news, having come from Palatka. My only other full-time employee during those two years was Bob Gleason, a good salesman/announcer. He was from a small town in upstate Alabama.

On one occasion, George Duck asked me to go to the courthouse and cover a rape trial that was being held. He had other chores to do in order keep us on the air. It seems the parents of a young lady from over in West Nassau County near a small hilly area known as Gobblers Knob were accusing some person of raping their daughter. I sat listening to the trial throughout and finally the verdict. Eagerly I rushed back to the station to put the big news on the radio. In a Walter Cronkite–type voice, I proudly reported that a certain person had been convicted of raping a young lady down in the gully near the Gobblers Knob. Somehow it didn't sound right when It came out over the airwaves on our evening news.

All this time, however, my thoughts more and more led me back toward the big city, where the big dollars in advertising were. It didn't take me long to realize that I had done more advertising on my four-hour show in Jacksonville than we were doing all day long on WFBF. We thoroughly enjoyed those two years at our first station, but I just couldn't shake the desire to get back to

Jacksonville. I still had that urge or longing for the big city where the real radio money was.

I had received a call wanting me and my band to perform at a Saturday night gig in Brunswick. It was the last time I would play for such an event. It was big dance being held at the Goodyear Homes Recreation Center. At some time during that evening, my two older brothers, John and Paul, got into a scuffle right down in front of me on the dance floor. I made up my mind that it was time for me to pack up my Rickenbacker steel guitar and my playing country music for ever. I had no regrets, however, because more and more all I thought about was radio, and being a successful radio-station owner.

In early 1957, while we were still at WFBF, my ultimate dream began to come true. A gentleman named Carmen Macri called me to ask if I would be interested in buying the daytime 1280 facility that had already been on the air for several months programming country music, because he was buying the full-time facility 1320, the *Jacksonville Journal* station where I had previously worked. At that time, the FCC would not let a person or entity own more than one facility. I jumped at the idea.

We sold our station in Fernandina Beach to a fellow from Philadelphia named Edward Murray who wanted to come south. Mr. Murray paid me $10,000 down, and the balance of $40,000 was to be paid over the coming years. I never got that money, because shortly afterward I had to repossess the station. I resold it at just over half the balance he owed me, just to get it off my hands. Meanwhile, I had used his $10,000 down payment to pay current bills and moving expenses, and to put our own down payment on a small house, because Carol did not want to move into another rental.

My father-in-law, Edison Casey, was impressed with what we had done with our Fernandina Beach station and wanted to be my partner in the future. Together, we bought WQIK 1280kc

1,000-watts daytime for $120,000. We put $20,000 down, and the balance was to be paid by a ten-year note to the former governor of Georgia, Ed Rivers.

The former owner of WQIK had already turned the station country and had filled the air shifts with country personalities I already knew, including Frank Thies, Glenn Reeves, and Butterball Bill Johnson. But the station was doing very little business. After FCC approval and the final closing, we took possession on July 1, 1957. To purchase my half ownership, I had borrowed my $10,000 for the down payment from my father-in-law's business partner, Clark Brown of St. Marys.

At the time, I had no idea what I was facing. I had the debt of having to pay Mr. Brown, plus I had to pay former governor Rivers a total of $1,800 a month. Right off, I wanted to move the tower over to west Jacksonville to improve our coverage, especially with the country-music audience. The current tower location was on a sand hill in the eastern part of Jacksonville known as Arlington, and it had very poor coverage. My determination to move the tower to the west side grew, and I knew that had to be my first major investment.

With a damned-if-I-do-and-damned-if-I-don't attitude, I relocated the tower to leased property off Twenty-First Street in West Jacksonville. Our business began to pick up immediately, as advertisers climbed aboard the growing WQIK—some of my former advertisers at WJHP along with new ones we picked up along the way. But I was burdened with debt. In addition to what I already was on the line to pay for, I now had to pay out approximately $10,000 cash to build a new tower and transmitter house and to move to our new location on the west side of town.

One day within the first three months of our operations, I got a lesson about advertising I was never to forget. A gentleman who identified himself as a concert promoter came into the station and told us he was bringing a show to Jacksonville. I had heard of him before, since he also owned a stock-car racetrack near Orlando.

The show would feature the Wilburn Brothers, Faron Young, and a young rising star, Loretta Lynn. I most definitely wanted WQIK to be a part of that show. I practically sold him the whole radio station for a full month for just $1,200. He agreed and opened his big fancy checkbook and gave me what I *thought* was a check for $1,200. *Hallelujah*, I thought. *I've finally got some money to help me pay my debts.*

Later that day, our bookkeeper and girl Friday, Dee Gordon, came to me and asked if I had looked at the check carefully. I said no. He looked to be an honest fellow, and he owned a racetrack, and he had a great show that we were going to help him promote. She explained that it was payable at the night of the performance and was not a check at all, even though it looked to be real and even had a bank's name on it.

I was really let down, but we dove in and promoted the dickens out of that show. Needless to say, on the night of the performance, that promoter could not be found. I had learned a hard lesson. Some years later, on a visit to Nashville, I spoke to Teddy Wilburn, and he told me none of them got paid either. I survived those first months, but I would never forget that promotion.

Within a short time after we had moved the tower to West Jacksonville, I was approached by the ACL Railroad to swap my twenty-year lease on the new tower-site property to them for a five-and-a-half-acre free and clear tract of land at the end of Rio Grande Avenue farther westward. It seems they wanted to run a spur railroad track through the property I had leased. Upon building a much taller tower at the new site, our signal improved even more, and WQIK was off and running—well on its way to becoming a major entity in the Jacksonville radio scene. Within a few months, we were grossing enough money for my wife and I to buy a larger house in Jacksonville, and with my confidence at an all-time high, I borrowed enough money from a bank to pay off my father-in-law plus the $10,000 I had borrowed from his partner.

We moved our offices and studios several times during those first years—one time to an office building on Eighth Street, then on Main Street, and even at one time on Adams Street in downtown Jacksonville. It was there that we gave firsthand coverage of the Roosevelt Hotel fire that occurred one New Year's morning, killing several people. Finally we built our studios at the Rio Grande location where our transmitter was located.

Indeed, those were years of being in radio-station ownership that I would cherish forever. Country music was beginning to be accepted more and more within the advertising community, and for the first time I began to feel prosperous. I never gave in to the temptation of going back to playing for a living. I was hell-bent on making WQIK the great success it is today. After paying off my father-in-law and his partner, I renegotiated my debt with former Gov. Rivers so I could pay him off too, but that left me with virtually no operating capital. I was living almost hand to mouth on my monthly cash flow.

At that time, my wife and I were firmly entrenched at Lakewood Methodist Church, where I had been baptized. I attended a men's Sunday school class with a teacher named Roscoe Buttry, who just happened to be president of a major Jacksonville bank. I have to admit, most of the time while he was teaching the men's class on Sunday mornings, I was not listening; I was thinking about how I could borrow money from his bank. Rather nervously one day, I decided to call him. He told me to come on in, which I did. After a few minutes' conversation, he sent me to a loan officer and said, "Let Rowland have the $20,000 he needs." I walked out of that bank the happiest person in Jacksonville, thinking that somebody up there really loves me.

After a couple of years on the air and being ambitious, I wanted nighttime or twenty-four-hour-a-day operations for WQIK, which was still daytime only. My consulting engineer told me that if I could find the acreage in northwest Jacksonville to put up four towers, I could get 1,000 watts at night on 1280kc. I drove around constantly for days in the northwest side of Jacksonville looking for ten acres or more of vacant land.

One day, I got the bright idea of hiring an airplane to take me up and fly over the area. From the air, I saw a large tract of land that was perfect for my proposed nighttime operation. As soon as we landed, I hurriedly got in my car and drove out to the area. Damn. It turned out to be a large cemetery with an undeveloped portion. I decided to give up on going nighttime and began concentrating more on improving our daytime facility.

Soon after moving the tower over to West Jacksonville, I got the itch again. Since I couldn't feasibly get nighttime, I decided to go up 5,000 watts and make the station more powerful. Previously, my father-in-law had objected to moving up in power until I made some money and had some operating capital in the bank. But I was doggedly determined to push WQIK to the top. Moving the tower to West Jacksonville was a great move, because I had paid off Mr. Buttry's bank, my father-in-law, and his partner all within my first two or three years of operations. Now I was ready to go to full power on 1280kc. But where would I get the money? I already had a quote of $18,000 for a new transmitter. Meanwhile, Mr. Buttry had left his bank to move back to Tennessee. Whom could I turn to for my expansion capital?

With all I had going on in my life, I found myself spending more time with my local attorney, Davison Dunlap. He suggested I try his bank, the Florida National Bank. I called the bank and talked to a loan officer who said, "Come up and see me."

On the day I was to meet the loan officer, I went to the bank in downtown Jacksonville and got on an elevator going up to the fifth floor with a short bald-headed gentleman whose name was Ed Ball. We chatted during our ride, and I told him who I was and what I was there for: to try to get a loan because I wanted to buy a new transmitter for WQIK. I explained how we had purchased the station and how it was growing. Just as he stepped off the elevator to go to his office, he turned to me and said, "Young man, go see loan officer Byrus Lee on the second floor and tell him I sent you."

After just a few minutes' conversation with Mr. Lee, I received a check for the $18,000 I needed. I walked out of the Florida National Bank that day thinking somebody up there really does love me. Little did I know that at the time, Ed Ball owned the bank and many more Florida National Banks throughout Florida, as well as the Florida East Coast Railway. He was one of the richest men in America. How amazing that I would get on the elevator with him of all people!

We soon installed the new 5,000-watt transmitter, and again WQIK began to make strides. But I wanted more for our station and country music. I applied for and received a permit to go to 50,000 watts on 1090kc. To do so was going to cost me over $75,000, which the equipment company financed. Once that equipment was installed, you couldn't hear it twenty-five miles north in Yulee, but we covered the east coast of Florida down to the Cape, and we had a near perfect signal over the northern Caribbean. In fact, for a few months, we broadcast a preacher on Sunday mornings with tape recordings from the Bahamas.

Later, after three years of high-powered operations with sky-high electricity bills and major breakdowns, we filed for and received a permit to move over to 1050kc with 5,000 watts, whereby we could get a 6:00 a.m. year-round sign-on time. After a few years under my ownership, our advertising sales had grown to $40,000 and sometimes as much as $50,000 a month.

About that time, I heard some rumors about the engineers in the area forming a union. That frightened me, because in those early days, all stations were required by the FCC to have at least one full-time fully licensed engineer on the payroll. Frank Thies had a first-class license, but I often worried about what we'd do if he left us. I'd be forced to hire a full-time person to just stand around and do nothing 90 percent of the time.

Then I got the bright idea of getting an engineer's license myself. Frank gave me a stack of papers with over 550 possible questions and answers about broadcasting electronics—in short, all of the elements needed to pass the FCC exam. I studied them for weeks, and then I went to Miami and passed the test with flying colors. I was still afraid of messing with those electronics and never opened the doors of a transmitter or any other equipment at WQIK. But I proudly hung my license on the wall, and today I still have it.

Usually once a month or more often, I would be in contact with my Washington FCC attorney, and he kept mentioning FM or frequency modulation and that I ought to consider it as a way to get on the air at night. It didn't appeal to me. AM radio was in my blood and perhaps the only thing I felt comfortable with. After a rather heated argument with him about the future of FM, as he called it, he talked me into sending him a check for $300 made out to the Federal Communications Commission as filing fees for the permit to operate an FM station on 99.1 in Jacksonville. I thought, *What the heck, I'll get the permit, but by the time I get the FCC permission I seriously doubt I will ever build it.*

I didn't realize that the FCC was really pushing FM, and we got the permit in no time. Things were going good for us in the late '50s and early '60s, so after a few months I decided to put the FM station on the air. I did, but I casually let my wife talk me into playing easy-listening music with the call letters WALZ. It lasted only three months.

I must admit, by that time my interest in FM was beginning to grow. More automobiles were coming out with FM on their radios, and the trade magazines were printing more and more stories about the rise of FM as the future of our medium. However, at WALZ with its easy-listening format, we did not sell one single commercial in three months. I began to get desperate, writing checks for electricity and manpower to keep it on the air.

I ask for and got permission to duplicate WQIK-AM during the daytime when it was on the air if I would keep the FM on the air until midnight or longer.

The day we began duplicating our country music on FM, I had a plan in mind. I would hire the best well-known country disc jockey available who also was a well-known former country singer and musician, Chuck Goddard, as my first nighttime FM personality, and for the first few nights I insisted that he keep a log of exactly how many phone calls we received for the opening night of country music on the air in Jacksonville after sundown. The response was overwhelming: over three hundred the first night, and it almost doubled each night for the next few nights. I knew we had hit pay dirt.

Later we would expand all-night operations into a twenty-four-hour operation with Big Jim Godbold. WQIK-FM would be a success, a rising star over the skies of Jacksonville. And I well remember the day I reluctantly sent my lawyer a check for $300 made out to the FCC for the permit. Today, it's worth millions. That event took place over fifty years ago.

Shortly after starting WQIK-FM as country station, I made a deal with a gentleman named Johnny Gordon, who was a salesman with an appliance distributorship on Liberty Street. I purchased five hundred small Chinese-built FM/AM radios for eight dollars each. We sold them over the air for fifteen dollars a piece. They were all gone within a few weeks. If poor people wanted to hear us and couldn't afford our radio, I'd give them one anyway.

One of our earliest promotions that helped put us on the map as a top facility in Jacksonville was working with the Jacksonville Jaycees or Junior Chamber of Commerce. My brother Bob had been in the organization for quite a while, hobnobbing with guys his age who would later become some of our best political leaders. They included Mayor Jake Godbold; Lynwood Roberts, the tax collector; Henry Cook, clerk of the court; and other well-known young men and their wives. They took over our entire radio station for a whole day once a year, selling and delivering their own advertisers, which hopefully raised a lot of money for their other efforts. Some of my regular advertisers didn't like the idea of being kicked off for a whole day, but it was a good promotion.

Jake Godbold, Mayor of Jacksonville and a friend of mine

When country-music radio was in its infancy, major national advertisers were hard to come by. For the first few years at WQIK, we existed mostly off of used-car dealers, transmission exchanges, mom-and-pop stores, and other local advertising. National advertisers—such as soaps, new cars, etc.—would not touch a country-music station.

I recall one occasion where I was almost thrown out of the office of an advertising "expert" for J. C. Penney stores in Jacksonville. He told me they didn't want *those people* in Penney's stores, because they had no money to spend. Thankfully, that image has long since gone, thanks to the efforts of the Country Music Association (CMA). But it did force us early radio-station owners to look elsewhere for ad dollars.

In the fall of 1958, I opened a letter from an advertising agency in South Florida. It stated that if I would take my unsold time and promote a new development called Cape Coral Homesites, they would pay me a dollar for each phone call they received asking for a brochure. I thought, *What the heck, let's try it.*

We did—we saturated the air with Cape Coral Homesites and urged our listeners to call and get their free brochure by simply dialing a toll-free number. We hit it hard, and I'm happy to say our listeners responded. Over the following weeks, we made over $3,500 from the ad begging our listeners to get their free brochure about Cape Coral Homesites. They responded, and I was able to pay a few bills with that money. I am not sure how many of our listeners bought a homesite in Cape Coral, but that was okay with me.

When the city of Jacksonville opened its big beautiful coliseum with seating for over fifteen thousand people in November 1961, the Reverend Billy Graham brought his weeklong Crusade to our city as its first event. One week later, we held our very first country-music show—we called it the WQIK Country Music Festival. To make certain it was a success, I and my agent in Nashville, Hubert Long, signed up every available act possible. I wanted to make certain it was talked about and made local headlines. I didn't know how I was going to pay for all that talent if it failed, but I had confidence in what we were doing, and I was enthusiastic about it.

I had signed Ray Price to be the headliner, along with Patsy Cline, Faron Young, Ray Pillow, Cowboy Copas, and several others. My cost for all that talent in 1961 was over $8,000. That was lot back then. Prior to beginning our advertising of the show, I met with the coliseum manager, Bill Lavery, and he suggested

I charge $10 a ticket. "Absolutely not," I insisted, and after much discussion we decided on the price of $2.50 each. More than the profits we would possibly make from the show, I wanted this event to go into the history books as a smashing success.

On the Saturday night of the event, the place was packed with people, even standing in some areas. Our gross was over $16,000. With the talent and the venue costs—including policemen, ticket printing and selling, everything—our expenses totaled approximately $13,000. It was a success, and I'll never forget how happy I was that night after the performance. My entire staff met me at an all-night pancake house where we celebrated. Afterward, when my wife and I got home, I told her, "Honey, don't tell anyone, but when I heard about our gross ticket sales, I peed in my pants."

The following Monday morning when I got off the air, I immediately called my agent. We picked a date in April 1962, and I told him to start looking for talent.

Another day in our early years at WQIK I will never forget is the day President John F. Kennedy was assassinated. I was in my attorney's office in downtown Jacksonville when suddenly his secretary burst into his office screaming, "The president has been shot!" This happened right after lunchtime. I immediately ran downstairs to my car and headed full speed for the radio station.

On the way to the station, I got on the two-way radio with our afternoon personality Frank Thies and asked him if he had been airing the news. His response was no. Our Associated Press wire was busted or something was wrong with it, because it wouldn't stop ringing. Neither Frank nor anyone else at the station knew that the constant ringing of the newswire was a signal of national importance in an emergency. I told him to do something, because CBS, NBC, and all the other network stations had announced that the president had been shot and was possibly dead. We couldn't go on playing honky-tonk music at a critical time like this.

Moments later, the networks announced that the president

was indeed dead, and I told Frank to announce it immediately. He stammered, as if he didn't know exactly what to say, or perhaps he did not believe me since I was out somewhere on my two-way radio. He just kept on playing his regular music and taking requests from folks on the telephone.

It was no more than fifteen minutes later that I arrived at the station and dashed into the control room, suddenly realizing that Frank was rather white in the face from the shock of not knowing what to do. I said, "This is bad, real bad," and after a few moments I decided to let the station go silent. Frantically I searched the Associated Press wire and got the story together, but I also realized we must first change the mood of our entire station for the rest of this day and perhaps the next. Beside our control panel we kept a small file of records, and without a second thought I grabbed a disc I felt to be appropriate for this terrible situation. Quickly, I put it on the turntable. It was a different-type disc, with two cuts on each side, by the Boston Symphony Orchestra. We used it regularly to sign on the station each morning. I flipped it over and immediately put the first cut on the air: "Stars and Stripes Forever" by John Phillip Sousa.

Frank and I starting putting ideas together about what we would do for the rest of that day and possibly on into the next. After all, we had never been in a situation like this before, and I'm sure we both were in some kind of shock from the fact that we had lost President Kennedy and didn't know what to do. To make matters worse, our Associated Press wire was bringing in more and more happening events by the minute. We simply couldn't digest it all at that moment in time.

Suddenly, we both realized the disc playing "Stars and Stripes Forever" had finished and had tracked over into the second cut and commenced to play a "whooping it up, happy day, hallelujah" version of "Dixie." At the split second the singers hit the second "hooray," I hit the turntable arm as hard as I could, knocking it out of commission for the rest of the day. I guess we both learned a lesson, and we promised not to panic if something of this importance ever came up again.

My business had prospered so much that my wife and I had purchased a big beautiful home in south Jacksonville. Our children would grow up in a house that we thought would be our permanent home. My wife stayed busy in the garden club, volunteering at Baptist Hospital, and with the various activities of our church. But most of all, she was making a good family for me and our children, something I had never known as a child.

Our first son, Marty, was six years old at the time. Ricky, our second son, was three, and Brian was born while we lived on San Sebastian Avenue. With so much happening in my life, it was hard for me to imagine the life I had some ten or fifteen years earlier up in Georgia, particularly the time I spent working at the dairy. Indeed, these were the best times of our married life due in part to the fact that I had resigned myself to always put my family first. At times, that was hard to do.

In 1959, my wife and I decided that in addition to our home in Jacksonville, we would build a beach house on Fernandina Beach, because we had made many friends living there after our years building WFBF. It was only a few miles from Jacksonville. We found a beautiful lot down near the golf course right on the ocean and paid $5,600 for it, and we spent just $28,000 for a sizeable oceanfront home. We financed our second home, but I had no trouble paying for it, as WQIK was really beginning to grow—plus our country-music concerts, which began in 1961, were always profitable.

At first we just visited the beach house on weekends. But after a year or so—and surviving a hurricane—the boys and I talked Carol into moving into it full-time. We quickly sold our San Sebastian Avenue home for a nice profit. We lived on the beach for only a year or two, after which we sold that house for a profit too. Living on the beach must have done something for my manhood, because our youngest son, Stephen, was born at that time. We later moved back to Jacksonville, but both of us still missed our friends in Fernandina Beach.

As a surprise to Carol one day, I called a realtor friend in Fernandina, John T. Ferriera, and bought a large tract of land just south of the golf course. Carol had always wanted a *Gone with the Wind*–type colonial home, and that's what we built. We lived there for five years, during which our children would grow up, and this would be their formative years.

We both loved the lifestyle and were content with the idea of living there for the rest of our lives. But it was not to be. Marty, as a young teenager, learned to play the drums with a rock 'n' roll band, and even though my wife dressed him properly for school and other events, he would stop on his way to the bus and hide his socks and go to school sometimes almost barefoot. In short, he gave us quite a lot of problems during that time, and we both became disenchanted with living in the area.

During the years we lived in Fernandina Beach, I was commuting to WQIK daily and once or twice a month to either WDEN in Macon, Georgia, or WQYK down in Tampa. One day, I noticed the local Chevrolet dealership had changed hands. For many years it was known as Woodward Chevrolet of Fernandina, and later it became Ken Lamb Chevrolet. At that time, between WQIK, my concert promotions, and our out-of-town stations—which were all really beginning to be profitable—I was terribly busy.

I casually mentioned to a friend at the dealership that I wish I had known it was for sale, because I would have liked to have bought it to give my family local ties to the community. Within a week I received a phone call from Gordon Thompson Jr. of Jacksonville, and in less than another week I was the proud owner of a Chevrolet dealership, without any previous knowledge or experience in the automotive business. I soon realized I'd made a tragic mistake.

Unlike a radio station, where it takes months to get a license, after signing the sales agreement it only took a few minutes to be in the car business. It happened so fast, I had little time to even think about what I was doing. The district manager of Chevrolet told me it was necessary for me to spend more than 50 percent of my time at the new Marshall Rowland Chevrolet. I told him that was impossible, but he urged me to sign the papers anyhow giving me the franchise.

With the feeling I could conquer any financial endeavor, I moved forward with the purchase. The price was less than $100,000, and the dealership appeared to be profitable, although I was not sure. I learned later that the monthly profit-and-loss statement was more than six pages long, and I didn't have time nor did I want to fully understand it. That was a costly error.

I intended to run the dealership like I had run my radio stations. I found a young fellow from South Georgia who had quite an attractive sales record at his father-in-law's business and appeared to honest and eager to manage a dealership on his own. I made him manager and turned the entire operation over to him.

Exactly one year and fourteen days later, I received a phone call from the president of the local Florida National Bank, Lewis Ferreira. He told me I needed to come over and put some money in the Chevrolet operating account. Thinking it was just a few dollars, I told Mr. Ferreira I would send my wife down to see him with maybe $500 or a $1,000. He muttered something and hesitated, and I asked him how much I needed to transfer. When he told me $42,000, I nearly fell out of my chair and on the floor at WQIK. I was flabbergasted.

I had just visited the dealership a few days before, and things appeared to be going fine. Little did I know that my new manager had bought thousands of dollars' worth of tires we would probably never sell because the salesman selling them gave him a set of four giant-sized tires for his dune buggy. And worse, little did I know that there were five brand-new Chevrolets—including two new Monte Carlos—running on loan all over the county, one of them for over a month. I also found out that in the week just passed, my manager had given GMAC, our floor planner, a bad $25,000 check because they said we were out of trust and they were going to come over and audit the dealership, which he did not want.

Without hesitation, I went to see my attorney, Davison Dunlap. I told him about the situation and asked him what was the worst possible thing that could happen to me if I just closed the dealership doors. He told me I could be sued by General Motors for the automobiles that were missing and the expenses on them, plus all the automotive parts that were missing and unpaid for, and that I might be responsible for the lease on the building.

I immediately made arrangements to pay every dime I owed to everybody including GMAC, the employees (even though I felt they too had plotted against me), and of course, the bank. I closed the dealership. That same day, GMAC sent a school bus full of drivers to Fernandina Beach, and they took every automobile off our lot, new and used, and drove them away while another truck hauled off all the parts on hand. I approached the manager and told him I was probably going to sue him for theft and everything else he had done wrong. He immediately told me I could not harm him, that he was a full-blooded Cherokee Indian and he was go back to the reservation where he could not be touched.

I suppose the thing that hurt me most about the automobile dealership was several months later, many friends we had sold Chevrolets to, sometimes below cost, would come up to me complaining about some minor nitpicking problem. Never again would I go into something as blind as I had just been through. On closing day, I went home and cried for three or four hours, and to this day I cannot tell you whether I was crying for joy that it was all over or out of sadness for closing up one of the major businesses in the town of Fernandina Beach. I think I might have gone out and gotten drunk if it hadn't been for my loving wife and family.

CHAPTER 4

OTHER RADIO STATIONS IN MY CAREER

Shortly after acquiring WQIK, I applied for and got a permit for a radio station in Douglas, Georgia. Why I chose that town to build my first out-of-town facility, I have no idea, but I suppose I was overanxious. I built it and put it on the air simply because someone had told me this was an ideal place to build a station for a rather small investment. It was WSIZ on 1310kc with 1,000 watts. Unfortunately, the owner of the existing station in the area didn't want any competition. He filed an extensive lawsuit against me with the FCC, full of trumped-up charges.

I got the license anyway, but it was temporary until the FCC could investigate and settle all his charges against me. A private inspector came down and spent a week at our station, researching and finding out all he could about my character. Finally, we settled after a year or so on the air. My competitor, Brody Timm, repaid me for all my out-of-pocket expenses, and I closed the station down as per our agreement. Confidentially, I was glad to get that turkey off my back.

In 1958, Carol wanted to go to Wesleyan College in Macon for her five-year class reunion. I gladly took her, but since I knew no one in the area and I certainly didn't want to go to an all-girls reunion, I had nothing to do but drive around in my car for two days listening to country-music stations from Atlanta. Later, after I was back in my office in Jacksonville, I told my Washington attorney Ray Paul about my trip to Macon and that I thought the area was ready for its own country-music station.

He suggested I file an application; after all, it would not cost that much to find out if I could get an AM station without going through what I previously endured in Douglas, the local competition trying to block me. I did. I filed for 1540kc with 1,000 watts. The FCC granted me a construction permit or license about four months later.

Before I even started building the station, my attorney called me again and said, "Hey Rowland, why don't you get an FM permit to go with your new station in Macon." Reluctantly I sent him a check for $300, and we received a permit for an FM on 105.3 for Macon to go with our day-timer on 1540kc—all of this before the AM station was even on the air.

This occurred just a few weeks after getting my permit for 99.1 FM in Jacksonville. I remember there were many times when I seriously doubted if I would ever build either one of them. AM radio to me was the only viable medium. But apparently the FCC really wanted to get FM up and running.

I spent a lot of time in Macon during the construction of the AM station, sometimes driving back and forth between Jacksonville and Macon, leaving home at five in the morning and returning at midnight that same day, and on other occasions spending a night or two in the area. After that, my manager and trusted friend Charlie Witt, who had been with me in Jacksonville for quite a while, handled everything to my satisfaction. That included our country-music promotions, since at the time Macon was also building a big new coliseum.

We immediately put WDEN-AM on the air, but waited for almost a year before deciding to build the FM I held a permit for. Just as I had experienced in Jacksonville earlier, the FM facility in Macon really began to prosper. I remember we seldom had a losing month as long as I owned those stations for almost seven years. I had given Charlie a small percentage of ownership in the stations and later, when we sold it, I paid him for his share and he stayed on with the new owners. Both the AM and FM had cost me less than $100,000 to build seven years earlier, and I sold them for almost four times that much several years later.

A few years later, after I had sold WDEN in Macon, an ex-employee of mine and a real good guy, Fred Newton, called and told me of a station I could buy near Macon, and perhaps move it closer to Macon and get good coverage over the area's population. I went up to the area, liked what I saw, and promptly gave the owner a $5,000 check as down payment. I agreed to purchase the station licensed to Gordon, Georgia, for only $35,000 (approximately).

I thought it was a good deal, but to my surprise, Fred—who was a good salesman and manager—changed his mind and was no longer interested, even though I had promised to give him part-ownership. He had a gotten a better position elsewhere. I had already signed an agreement to purchase the station, so I had to go through with it or forfeit my $5,000 deposit.

I had the feeling this was going to be a challenge, but I didn't how big that challenge would be. Finding a program niche and relocating the tower nearer to Macon was indeed to become futile, or at least less than rewarding.

I finally found a tower site on top of a hill about three miles east of Gordon, and we promptly got permission put the tower up. My engineer Don Jones was with me to help with the transmitter move. At that time, to save money, we depended on satellite transmissions to our station from a broadcast-programming company in Dallas, Texas. One day, just after we had built the tower and constructed a huge eight-foot-tall dish to receive satellite programming at the base of the tower, a local log truck or pulpwood driver was passing by when the driver suddenly slammed on his brakes. He came over to Don and asked him what it was. The big round dish was indeed odd looking, sitting out there in the woods next to the highway.

Don explained it was our receiver for a satellite twenty-two miles up in the air that we would be rebroadcasting programs from. The fellow then asked him how that satellite would get its electric power. Don, being kind of a practical joker himself, explained that just over the next hill, if you looked closely, you could see a long, long extension cord running from a telephone pole on the ground up to the satellite twenty-two miles up in the sky, feeding the satellite with electricity.

The fellow left shaking his head in total amazement, and I believe he really took Don's story seriously, not knowing whether to believe him or not. To this day I am not sure of how many people he told about the programming on WIZY-FM in the Gordon, Georgia, area.

WQYK-AM and FM in Tampa/St. Petersburg was an entirely different situation. At a Florida Association of Broadcasters meeting in Daytona, I met a fellow named Bob Weeks who, with his partner Jim Walter of the home-building world, had purchased a real powerful daytime AM station on 1110kc. I casually told Bob at that broadcasters meeting that if they ever decided to sell the station, I would be interested, because being as powerful as it was it would make an ideal country-music operation. Less than two weeks later, I received a phone call from Jim Walter himself, and he asked that I come down to Tampa and talk to him about the station.

His office was on the top floor of a big building on Dale Mabry Street, and I certainly remember that office because it was almost as big as my entire home. Once I arrived and sat down, he pulled out a humidor, and we both lit up giant Cuban cigars. Man, I was in hog heaven. In short, I had arrived at the big time.

After some discussion, we worked out a deal whereby I was

to buy 49 percent of his station until his three-year tenure with the FCC was over. At that time, I was to buy the remaining 51 percent and have full ownership of the station. The purchase price was $300,000, with me paying him the $49,000 down and the balance of $51,000 due to him at closing eighteen months down the road. His bank in Tampa would finance the remaining $200,000 for the station. At the moment he presented the contract, I was so excited I would have signed anything he put in front of me. He was indeed a very wealthy man and an honorable person.

The station was apparently losing money as an easy-listening station prior to my involvement, and even when I turned it to country music, I had to put money into it almost every month. After a year and half of struggling with the station against a very good local country-music competitor, I went to Mr. Walter and told him I could not pay him $51,000 for his 51 percent ownership share. I suggested he sell me 1 percent and we remain 50/50 partners. He thought for a moment and said, "I have a better idea."

With that, he pushed a button calling his lawyer in the next room to join us. Without hesitation, he told his attorney to dig up the note I had signed for $51,000 and tear it up, and "Give Rowland 100 percent of the station." I was overwhelmed with his kindness; I could not believe someone would do this for me. I had spent so much time worrying over how I would get the money to pay him off, and all I had hoped for was a 50/50 proposal. I left his office that day with a sigh of relief, full of thankfulness to him. Indeed, Jim Walter was my kind of man.

Within a few weeks of obtaining full ownership of WQYK-AM, I heard about a high-powered FM classical-music station in downtown St. Petersburg on a 100-foot tower operating out of someone's backyard that had been shut down for some reason. I checked it out and found out it could be bought for the expenses, which were about $90,000. After arranging a loan with the Sun Bank in Jacksonville, my attorney Ellis Neder and I went to the closing. We appeared before the judge and purchased the station.

I quickly found out why the station had been shut down: it seemed like the owner owed everybody in town. All day long I was writing out checks to various ex-employees, to the electric-power company, and to many other people in the area. I took the station off the air, and within weeks I found a tower site out off Gandy Boulevard that covered both Tampa and St. Petersburg. We began to prosper almost immediately. My brother Bob and his wife Gwen promptly moved to Tampa and took over the operation. We had many good employees at WQYK-AM and FM, including Don Hibbitts as sales manager and Jim Malloy as program director.

Back at home, after my debacle in the auto-ownership busi-ness, my wife and I felt it best to move from Fernandina Beach. We sold our home there, and I decided to swap jobs with Bobby. He came to Jacksonville to run WQIK-AM and FM, and my wife and I moved Tampa to run WQYK. However, shortly after our move, my wife decided she did not like living in the area. She was a homebody and wanted to be near her family and friends in Jacksonville.

The station continued to grow, and I wound up selling it to Bill Edwards from Houston, Texas, for $1 million in 1977. He paid me $250,000 down and the balance over ten years. He had owned a country station in Houston and knew better than I the value of what I had. And to prove it, just a few years later he sold it for over $30 million cash. He still owed me the balance of his mortgage, which I received. My children and I regret very much selling the stations in Tampa. You win some and you lose some, and not all decisions will be the correct ones. That has proven to be the worst financial move I would ever make.

Looking back at my many trips and the time we spent living in Tampa, there's one event I will never forget. There was a small daytime station just south of Tampa in Sarasota. When I first started visiting the area, I would listen to it in amazement. I thought the person running that station must be some kind of a weirdo. Instead of selling advertising like I had done all my life and like most of the radio stations in America were doing, he had a different idea.

He would go out to a merchant or business and give them the advertising on his station in exchange for certificates that could be redeemed for merchandise at their business. For instance, he would go to a Kentucky Fried Chicken place and swap them advertising for fifty gift certificates each for a bucket of chicken, and then he would come back and sell the certificates at auction over his station. Many times when I was listening to his station, I thought he should be banned from the airwaves and his license taken away from him.

His name was Lowell Paxson, and how wrong I was about this man. Later in life I would meet him, and I learned that he started the Home Shopping Network on television nationwide and became a multi-multi-millionaire, starting with that idea at his station in Sarasota.

At some time in 1977, my oldest son, Marty, had gone to work over in Albany, Georgia, for a radio station, and he was telling me what a good market it was. We applied for an FM channel for Leesburg, Georgia, adjacent to Albany, and got it. I later added a second station with a license to Sasser, Georgia, near Albany. We operated them both, WJAD-FM and WEGC-FM, out of the same studios in downtown Albany.

Unfortunately, we could not find a format that would attract the folks in Albany. With a format of soft rock on one and country on the other, the stations did not sell well with local advertisers. They did break even, though, and were not a drag on my other resources. I had built two towers for them, and the completed radio stations ran to a total cost of approximately $250,000. I sold WJAD-FM and WEGC-FM for just over $500,000 to a local furniture dealer who wanted to get in the business. I had overlooked one thing: a large percentage of the Albany area had a minority population who didn't care for either country or soft rock.

When my son Brian was about to graduate from Florida State University in Tallahassee, we heard of an FM channel available in a nearby area that would cover all of metro Tallahassee. We filed for it and got it. It became WQHI-FM on 99.9, and we went on the air in December 1988. The station was self-sustaining, and Brian did an excellent job of playing what I thought was soft rock with a large appeal to the college crowd. Unfortunately for him and his wife, I was forced to sell the station by the First Union Bank at an early date, for I had gotten way over my head in debt. Our country was going through a recession, and interest rates were sky high. We sold it at nice profit, but I was not to see any of the money from that sale.

When I sold WQIK in June 1984, a part of the sale was a non-compete agreement for any broadcasting by me within twenty-five miles of Jacksonville. Itching to get back in the business, I found a station for sale that was located just over thirty-five miles away in St. Augustine. I investigated and felt it would be a good place for my wife and I to relocate, since our sons were all grown and no longer living at home. I bought WSOS, a low-power FM, in early 1985 from Jim Martin and his partner. My wife and I bought a beautiful condo overlooking the marina where I kept my boat. I'm not certain my wife enjoyed it as much as I did. We were very active in the area and made a lot of friends, but somehow she never felt at home.

While living in St. Augustine, I got hooked on offshore fishing. I had already owned a thirty-six-foot boat I kept either in Jacksonville Beach or Fernandina Beach, but nothing like Camanche Cove Marina, where my wife and would spend the last eighteen years of our lives together. Today I have many trophies and awards and pictures adorning my walls from my fishing days with some of my best friends for life. Living in St. Augustine and being involved in offshore fishing competitions while owning one of the two radio stations in town made me feel on top of the world. We were always welcomed in the community and felt a part of it.

In 1986, my boat *The Station Break* won the annual tournament, and my crew and I got a free round-trip ticket to Hawaii for a week where we fished in the IBT or International Billfish Tournament. On the last day, off the big island of Hawaii, we hooked a 370-pound yellowfin tuna. The crew running the charter boat insisted I take the rod for this hookup. I did, and after over three hours of battling the monster, we finally boated it. I was dog-tired and even suggested releasing the tuna while I was fighting it. The charter guys said no way, they wanted to sell the meat after that day was over for the extra money. I kept on rockin', rollin', and reelin' and finally brought it in.

On one of our offshore trips out of St. Augustine, we found a Jet Ski floating sixty-five miles offshore, and it looked almost new. We circled it for a bit while I called the Coast Guard asking for information. They told me if possible to pull it ashore, and we had to pull it very slowly, arriving back at the marina around ten o'clock that night.

I did not contact the Coast Guard again, but in a couple of weeks two young guys from Miami drove up to claim it. They had reported their Jet Ski as lost. Apparently they were just off Miami Beach a good distance out in the ocean and ran out of gas. They left it and went to get gas, and when they came back it had drifted out of sight. I told them I wanted $500 for pulling it in. They refused and went back to Miami. Trying to sell a salvaged boat or other item you have taken in from offshore is almost impossible, and I wound up giving the danged thing away to a friend of mine up in Georgia who lived on a private lake.

St. Augustine was a wonderful place to live, but as a radio-station market, it wasn't very easy. My competition had been there for many years, and in addition he did a lot of trading for his advertising, whereby he would take merchandise instead of cash. I couldn't pay my payrolls and electric bills with merchandise.

As the nation's oldest city, St. Augustine is basically a tourist town, attracting millions of visitors a year. It's a town with lots of fine restaurants, things to do, and places to go, but in 1985 it did not have its share of commercial businesses like department stores and appliance dealers. It did have automobile dealers, but they wanted their extra business to come from Jacksonville, which we did not cover.

Still, building and operating WSOS on 105.5 was a fun challenge. My sons Rick, Brian and Stephen all loved the area and worked at our new venture. We added an AM station on 1170 licensed to St. Augustine Beach, and for a while we did tourist-information programming on it. I received quite a write-up in the national magazine *Entrepreneur* about our idea of visitor-information radio. It was unique, but I always felt it was successful because the area got several million visitors each year.

After five years of good times with WSOS-FM, I was approached by a fellow from Tampa about buying the station. I sold it to him and his backers for almost the same amount I had invested in it. I still miss the fun times in the ancient city.

In 1988, I got involved in a prolonged hearing whereby the winner was to receive a low-power 3,000-watt FM for Marco Island, Florida. Prior to the recession our country was in, you could get an FM permit and license just about anywhere in a major market or city for a few hundred dollars. Now, however, such a license was an extremely valuable commodity, and certainly the Naples/Marco Island area was no exception.

There were several applicants for the available FM frequency, and with me feeling my oats from the success of the Jacksonville, Macon, and Tampa radio stations along with the country-music concerts, I was able to purchase or pay all of the applicants for their expenses to drop out ... except one. I made an agreement with him where I would buy 49 percent and he would sell me the remaining 51 percent after the station had been on the air for three years. That was another costly error.

The station virtually broke me while I was getting a license that cost me over $300,000 in legal fees and buy-outs. By the time we got on the air, I had spent another $250,000 building the facility. When we first went on the air in 1991, I began to realize that I was in the middle of a giant poker game with high stakes, and there was no way out except to hang on and pray.

My son Stephen went to Naples to sell advertising. My son Rick, who was an engineer/announcer, went to Naples, where he and a young lady named Claudia Gomez made up the staff of totally automated WGUF, a 3,000-watt station on the FM dial. The three of them were able to gross enough money to pay the local expenses, but not nearly enough to pay the hundreds of thousands of dollars it took to get the license to build it and go through the legal wrangling I did with the FCC.

I sold the station in 1994 to my friend Jim Martin for just over $400,000, and I figure I lost well over $1 million in the entire process. I got so desperate to sell the station that I convinced myself that if I could possibly get rid of this huge lemon, it might add a year or two to my life. I simply did not have the resources or the will to keep the station and develop it into a profitable facility. *Never again*, I thought.

Meanwhile, I had also contracted with my father-in-law's wife, Lois, to buy her FM station licensed to St. Marys, Georgia. We received FCC permission to relocate the license to Callahan, Florida, and move the tower closer to Jacksonville. Since my noncompete covenant with the buyers of WQIK had expired, I was able to build WAIA-FM on 93.3 in 1990. For the first year, we programmed traditional country music but had minimal success.

Jacksonville had two high-powered country stations at the

time. The old great country music at that time was going out of style, so we later went to a rock format and called it the Party Pig, and it was self-sustaining as long as we owned it. After four or five years of operating the station, I sold it to Lowell Paxson, the gentleman I mentioned earlier who started the Home Shopping Network.

With the sale of WSOS-FM St. Augustine and the sale of both Tallahassee 99.9 FM and Jacksonville 93.3 FM, and after getting way over my head in debt to First Union Bank and just barely avoiding bankruptcy, I was glad to put all of the smaller stations I had ventured into in those smaller out-of-town markets behind me. At this point, I began to think about perhaps getting out of radio entirely and maybe even beginning a new career.

I gave much thought to my first love of country music as a musician, playing my steel guitar, or as a promoter. I considered buying a building and running a Grand Ole Opry–type theater in Jacksonville. I guess my early years of both music and radio successes had made me greedy or had given me the feeling that I could conquer the world, and now my age was beginning to make me realize I was not at all invincible.

While the above ups and downs in my broadcasting career between 1975 and 1995 were taking place, Lady Luck popped her head up and smiled upon me and my family. My son Marty had discovered a real winner for us to take a good look at, and as luck would have it, that turned out to be one of my best ventures. It was a high-powered FM channel on a relatively low tower in downtown Waycross, Georgia, on 102.5 FM and with 100,000 watts. My consulting engineers had told me that by erecting a 1,050-foot tower almost halfway between Brunswick and Waycross, we would cover both markets.

We contracted with a company from Kentucky to build my highest tower ever, the 1,050-foot tower near Lulaton, Georgia. I spent several days just watching these fellows at work and almost wound up going to the hospital with a bad crick in my neck from staring upward into the sky. Meanwhile, we had built new studios just east of Brunswick on Highway 80 to house these and perhaps other facilities if we ever expanded our operations there.

We later we purchased another 100,000-watt station in the area on 103.3 WHFX. The FCC now permitted a person or other entity to own several stations in one market. I made an agreement with Mr. Jim Rivers, the owner of WHFX-FM, to purchase it for just over $1 million. I had the down payment he requested, but I did not have the financing in place.

When I went to sign the contracts, Mr. Rivers balked at the signing, saying he would only sell the stations provided I would let his bank finance the balance. Again I looked up and thought to myself, *the Lord is taking care of me.* My financing worries were over and my prayers were answered. Shortly after buying 103.3, we also acquired the aged WMOG 1490 AM, and its FM on 93.7 came with it. All four of these stations were built into great radio local-area facilities with my son Marty as manager and my son Brian as programmer. They always made money with very few problems.

Beginning in 1986 until a few years later, WBGA was a stand-alone country music station. Adding WHFX 103.3 plus the WMOG-AM and FM to our operations brought new programming and sales problems, but nothing we couldn't handle. Putting these four stations together under one roof while cutting operating costs with automation and satellite usage was indeed very profitable. To this day, I still regret selling them to Root Communications of Daytona Beach, but after all I had been through with radio stations in town and out of town, and all the financial ups and downs I had gone through in recent years, I felt it really was time for me to retire and for my four sons to seek their future and fortunes elsewhere.

I figured that by selling the Brunswick stations for $5,450,000, I could pay all my debts, leave something to my sons, and still have enough to retire on. As fate would have it, about two weeks after the sale was closed, on April 1, 1998, a student pilot flying a military fighter jet from Moody Air Force Base hit the 1,050-foot tower near Lulaton, taking the stations off the air for a while. Thank goodness I had already invested the money and they couldn't get it back and perhaps cancel the sale.

As I look back over my radio career, which stretched from my first station in Fernandina Beach in September 1955 until I sold the last ones in Brunswick/Waycross in 1998, I feel much pride but also some deep regret. I regret very much selling the stations in Tampa/St. Petersburg, Macon, Brunswick/Waycross, and of course WQIK, my home station in Jacksonville. WQIK was the station that provided the drive, the finances, and the spirit for me go out and develop all the others. I can look back and realize the mistakes I made along the way, but I know that I also made many friends for life and wound up with a great retirement.

CHAPTER 5

LOOKING BACK AT MY SIXTY YEARS OF RADIO DAZE

From the day I built my first radio station in Fernandina Beach, Florida, I realized I had to surround myself with good reliable employees, have a good frequency, and come up with plenty of good ideas to make it a success. As I worked my way deeper into broadcasting, I kept an eye out for good reliable people who, whether or not they were as in love with country music as I was, would make a good contribution to my efforts.

Bill Mize started as a salesman at WQIK, and later I made him manager. He was a football referee and great old Alabama boy with a wonderful wife and family. When I sold the station in 1984, part of the sales agreement was to make certain he would stay with the organization. I'm sure WQIK would have been much harder for me to manage without Bill.

Charlie Witt was another great manager and, later, partner of mine. When I received the permit for a new station in Macon, Charlie and his family moved there. The rest is history in middle Georgia.

I had known Frank Thies even before he joined WQIK. In fact, Frank was on the air at the station when we purchased it.

He was known for communicating with people and his love of country music. Frank and I worked together for over thirty-five years. His drive-time show in the evening and later years as part of our morning team always brought good ratings.

We brought in Neil Linton to join him in the mornings. Frank and Neil were a natural for several years and did a great job. Their brand of humor was really a crowd-pleaser. During their time together in the mornings, WQIK became one of the top-billing radio stations in gross advertising sales in town. Neil, however, let prosperity go to his head, and I had to fire him for not showing up for an important broadcast and other not-being-cooperative events. After I paid him his last-month's salary, he went out into our parking lot and cried for several hours.

My son Brian was programming the station at the time and had become friends with a fellow named Boomer who was on a rock station at night. Boomer joined us at WQIK. Since he was younger than Frank, they bantered back and forth, and he would become firmly entrenched as a top morning personality for many years. They were joined in later years by a youngster named Gregory Gaines.

I got a call one day from my brother Bob and his wife, Gwen, who had built their own radio station in Vero Beach, telling me he was about to lose a good employee and was I interested? That was Gregory Gaines, and it seems he had a young child with a serious liver problem and it was important that he move near Gainesville, Florida, to have the child under the care of Shands Hospital.

One of the mandates the FCC required of radio licensees at the time was that a certain percentage of our employees must be minority. Greg was a well-educated black man; most of our listeners did not know it because it didn't matter. He really put a spark in our morning team. The three of them—Boomer, Frank, and Greg—went on to obtain our best listener-survey ratings ever and our highest advertising rates ever. I remember that because we received our first contract for over $10,000 at $150 per ad.

Many times we would air these new, more expensive commercials adjacent to the local advertisers who paid merely four dollars per advertisement.

I often rewarded my employees by taking them on trips to the Bahamas on our company-owned boat, the Station Break. Over the years, I had owned many boats, from a thirty-five-foot Bertram to a forty-five-foot Hatteras. I remember one trip where Sabrina, our news girl, was with us. She wore her life jacket and read the Bible all the way across the ocean to the Bahamas and back. Apparently, she couldn't swim.

At some time in the early years at WQIK, I was selected to be Mr. DJ, USA, by WSM in Nashville. I went to Music City, was on the Ralph Emory all-night show, and the next day stood on the stage of the Grand Ole Opry in the Ryman Auditorium, where Roy Acuff introduced me and talked about WQIK in Jacksonville, Florida, to the radio audience on WSM 50,000-watt 650 AM and to the packed house on hand that night at the Opry. I truly loved being an on-air personality, but I had to give it up early on because of the time spent managing our operations.

In the late '70s, we came up with one of our best all-time promotions, giving us national publicity. It was called "the Good Old Boy of the Day." Each day we would select a letter from listeners or make our own decisions and select such a person. Many times during the day, we would salute that individual and have things to say about them. Even though the promotion was rather chauvinistic in nature because it appealed only to men, it got us much publicity.

Ronald Reagan came to Jacksonville and spoke to the Northside Business Men's Club, and afterward we presented him with our "Good Old Boy of the Day" baseball cap. When he was later elected president, on the day he took office, we ran a full-page in the *Florida Times Union* with a picture of him holding that baseball cap with the words underneath, "Welcome to our Country, Mr. President."

President Reagan gets our Good Ole Boy of the day award

Mayor Jake Godbold was also a recipient. I had editorialized for him, something I had never done before. In fact, that editorial almost got me run out of town by his opponent when the mayor ran for reelection. Some years later, while in office, Mayor Godbold appointed me to the Jacksonville Sports Authority, an organization he had formed to bring a pro-football team to our city.

During the time I was in Tampa operating WQYK and my brother Bobby was managing WQIK in Jacksonville, he called to tell me about a fellow who came into his office and wanted to do the insane thing of giving airplane traffic reports in the morning and evening drive times. At first I thought Bobby was joking, but he was serious and had already figured out the cost of leasing a plane for the two or more hours a day it would be needed, plus he had spoken to several advertisers about the idea. In fact, he had already hired the guy who was a pipefitter on the new Prudential building, Robbie Rose, to do those reports.

I gave the go-ahead, and rest is history. Robbie would go on to become an icon over Jacksonville with his airplane and his way of describing traffic conditions. He was an overnight hit in broadcasting for our area—so much that after a few months, we bought our own plane, a loop-de-loop Cessna Aerobat airplane. Immediately after we began to make waves with Robbie at our daytime-only facility, two full-time stations would follow our idea and put airplanes up there in the skies over town. That took the wind out of our advertising sales.

One day, Robbie reported to me that the nose cone had fallen off the Cessna Aerobat somewhere over downtown Jacksonville. The possible liability that could occur from something like this and the loss of advertising dollars to our new competitors caused us to discontinue his flying. Robbie would remain an on-air personality in Jacksonville, and people loved him.

While Robbie was with WQIK, a well-known lady who happened to be a big WQIK fan called and asked if I would have Robbie strew her late husband's ashes out over the ocean. Robbie agreed and met the lady, her daughter, and Mayor Godbold's assistant at the airport. At the same time, a big black limousine delivered her husband's remains in a little black plastic bag. They all boarded the plane, and Robbie flew them just offshore.

He opened a small ventilation window up front in the cabin and tried to scatter the remains—but to his dismay, the ashes flew back into the plane all over everyone. Instantly, Robbie shoved the bag with its contents out the window and closed it. Upon landing and unloading the plane, they all looked up and there on the guy-wires at the tail of the plane hung the little black bag with its contents.

Robbie Rose, one of Jacksonville's more famous radio personalities, is shown here with Judge Dorcas Drake and Frank Thies at her annual Christmas giveaway for children

Frank Thies was with me the day I bought the WQIK in July 1957, and he was with me until I sold it. Although originally an engineer, he gradually became one of Jacksonville's top radio personalities. Frank ventured out on his own on several occasions and left us. At one time he owned a restaurant, then a bar, and once he even moved to the country to raise chickens. The dreams he pursued never seemed to develop and seldom lasted more than a few months. Frank knew he was always welcome back at WQIK, and I was always glad to have him return.

He was singled out many times by the country-music stars who would come to Jacksonville for our shows or concerts. Jimmy Dean, Roy Clark, Bill Anderson, Slim Whitman, and Glenn Campbell all dropped in to visit with Frank and chat on the air when they were near Jacksonville.

Several times Frank and I would talk about religion. Frank was steadfast in his beliefs as an agnostic. There were parts of the Bible he just could not believe. He had come to the conclusion there was a supreme being, but he wasn't sure.

Several years after I sold WQIK and he had retired, Frank bought a motor home and wanted to travel across America. It was in this motor home that he died while out west. When his wife, Alta, called to tell me Frank had died, I was fishing a tournament off Daytona Beach. She told me he had suffered a stomach hemorrhage at the foot of Mount Rushmore in South Dakota. She asked if I would mind speaking at his funeral. Of course I agreed to.

The day of his funeral arrived and I thought I was prepared, but that was not so. The building was full of people, but much to my surprise I was the only person up front on the lectern looking down upon his body and then out over the audience. There was no music, no ministers or other speakers. *What have I gotten myself into?* I thought. *I am not capable or qualified to speak at a person's last rites.*

I really called upon the Lord to help me in this situation. I asked God to give me something good to say about Frank and soothe his family. I told about the thousands of people Frank had made happy daily by riding home with them and communicating with them on the radio over the forty years he was on the air in Jacksonville. I must have talked for fifteen or twenty minutes, sharing every good thing I could think of about Frank. I asked the audience to bow their heads in a moment of silence for Frank. I finished by pouring out everything on my mind in prayer for him.

A similar incident happened a few years later when Glenn

Reeves passed away. Glenn had worked for us off and on for many years, had recorded for Decca records, and in addition had a regional television show carried on many stations throughout the south. Glenn died from cancer after being crippled some years earlier in an auto accident.

Since he had told me in our earlier days together that his mother was a minister, I assumed someone would be on hand to conduct his funeral service when his wife, Jeannie, asked me to speak. I wanted to make certain someone would be there for his last rites other than just me, as had happened at Frank's funeral. Not so, and I made a silent vow to myself to never ever let this happen to again. I renewed that vow to myself later when some folks told me his wife had recorded my words and had played my efforts on tape for several folks. Upon hearing of this, I didn't know whether to be flattered or floored.

Many different radio personalities came and went over my years at WQIK. One person in particular who made a big difference in our programming was Rusty Walker. He left us after a couple of years to become a nationwide program director for country-music stations across America. Tony Kitt was another great personality who worked mostly at nighttime on our station. Last I heard, he was with a top station in Atlanta.

Others who made my life and job as owner and operator easier were Frieda Prince and later Ann Mullis. They were my secretaries and financial assistants for many years, but more than that they were the glue that kept our organizations running by giving me reports on a regular basis of our various operations. Frieda became invaluable during the days of our country-music concerts. She left the radio station to go into real estate, where I understand she has done quite well.

I'm certain I have left out other important employees who helped make the station successful, but the folks I have mentioned in this book were the mainstays or the cornerstones of our successful operations.

On a few occasions, my wife, Carol, would come and help out. She had majored in broadcast journalism at Wesleyan College in Macon. For our twenty-fifth anniversary in 1982, I wanted to do something very special. Our team of Frank and Neil was among the top-rated morning shows in Jacksonville. Carol and I came up with the idea of a twenty-fifth-anniversary April Fool's calendar featuring Frank and Neil. After all, their show was full of humor and wit along with the country music.

**A shot from our Christmas calendar promotion
showing Frank and Neil up to their antics**

Carol worked diligently getting costumes prepared and spotting locations to make a production of this anniversary event. It was a huge success, and for each month of the year she would present a different picture featuring Frank and Neil in different comedy situations. It wound up costing us several thousand dollars, but it was a huge success, and we gave away several thousand of them for our twenty-fifth anniversary.

In November 1982, because of my public recognition and involvement in community affairs, I was selected by the Spina Bifida Association to be roasted by other leading personalities in the area. The young lady behind all of this was Suzanne Cato. In years prior, she had raised a great deal of money for the organization, and apparently she felt roasting me would do the same. I had never been roasted publicly (maybe privately), so it was rather exciting that I would be chosen from all of Jacksonville for that honor.

Suzanne went to work lining up other personalities, and I put out the word in Nashville about the event. The auditorium of the Hilton was packed with folks paying premium prices for dinner. A picture elsewhere in this book shows all the roasters who poked fun at me. Jerry Clower said I was even qualified to live in Mississippi.

However, some of the roasting was not aimed at me. It seems that Mayor Godbold and my old boss man from the dairy, Pete Gibson, who was then head of the Okefenokee Rural Electric System in Georgia, were both claiming rights to the northern parts of Duval County, and friendly fireworks starting flying between them. But Pete did go on and remind all those in attendance that evening about my four years of cleaning the milking barn, hauling out the fertilizer, and bottling milk way back when I was only twelve years old. In fact, he said that sometimes I got more fertilizer above my toes than just 'tween them.

Mae Axton, Bobby Bare, and Jerry Clower were also present

that night. Another political figure, Henry Cook, drew a caricature of me for the opening of channel 7's televising of the event,
and I'm proud to use it for the cover of this book. Quite naturally,
we broadcast the event on WQIK. It was truly a highlight of my
life, and I'm proud to say it raised about $25,000 for the Spina
Bifida Association and its good works. The *Florida Times Union*
had several stories in the days following.

What I have written in this book should give readers an idea
of what it takes to be successful, whether in a country-music
station or almost any endeavor. As far as I'm concerned, it takes
the efforts of many wonderful, dedicated people to make a dream
like the one I have lived over my lifetime come true. I still look
back with pride at my many years of ownership and the success
of my stations. Besides the fertilizer 'tween my toes, I have always
believed in using good old common horse sense and plenty of
hard work.

I sold WQIK in June 1984 for $3,250,000. I gave my existing
employees $1,000 each for every year they had been with me. I
didn't have to do that, but I wanted them to know how much they
meant to me. That amounted to over $65,000, and after paying
all my debts I still had enough left over for retirement at the early
age of fifty-five.

That retirement didn't last, and I would buy and sell more
stations in the years to come. But no doubt about it, WQIK was
the closest to me of all my stations and probably the most profitable over my lifetime. It gave me a position in the community and
provided all of the advertising necessary to promote our many
concerts in Jacksonville and make them profitable. On the day
I sold it in July 1984, my wife cried all through the closing. The
attorneys had to take her into another room to have her sign
certain documents.

Many exciting events occurred during our twenty-eight
years of ownership of WQIK. One was an invitation to visit with

President Gerald Ford. He was up for reelection, and I suppose he wanted our support. Other Florida broadcasters and my wife and I met with him for a couple of hours in one of the rooms of the White House. The only thing I remember about meeting with him was that he needed dental work.

To Carol and Marshall Roland
With best wishes;

Gerald R. Ford

Carol and I meeting President Ford in the White House

My desire to own an airplane stayed with me over the years at WQIK. I remember talking my employee friends Glenn Reeves and Frank Thies and my brother Bobby into buying another airplane with me for only $1,400 at a local airport. I went to the Florida National Bank, and they loaned me the $1,400 with monthly payments of $180. Each of us was to pay our share of the loan plus our share of expenses of flying the plane, an Aeronica Champ two-seater.

Frank had had some previous flying experience but had never soloed. After two months, Glenn dropped out of paying his share, and the next month Frank said his wife was going to divorce him if he didn't get out of that damn airplane. I could tell Bobby was less than excited over having to pay his share as well. So after only a few months, I sold the plane.

A likely purchaser came along, and on the day he came for a test flight, I pointed out to him that the fuel tank was right behind our head and the gauge on it had developed a slight leak, saturating the cloth behind us with a high-octane fuel smell. We went out and flew over Jacksonville, and right over downtown Jacksonville I glanced over at him as he was lighting a cigarette. I turned white I'm sure, because if that high-octane fuel smell had been ignited when he lit that cigarette, we'd have both been goners. This made me lose any desire for owning another airplane.

CHAPTER 6

COUNTRY-MUSIC CONCERTS—IN MY BLOOD

When the city of Macon, Georgia, built a big beautiful coliseum, our country-music format on the new WDEN in the late '50s and early '60s fit right in. On Friday nights, our concerts sold almost as many tickets as we did in Jacksonville on Saturday nights. The Curtis Hixson Hall in downtown Tampa was the venue we used while we owned WQYK, and all of our country shows were scheduled there on Sunday afternoons.

The Friday, Saturday and Sunday lineup really attracted the Nashville agents as well as their talent. On many occasions, I would travel with the stars from one town to another. Sometimes my wife and children would travel with us, and sometimes I did it alone. Even though my wife and I moved to Tampa in 1971 for just over two years, it didn't stop me and my show promotions.

One day while I was running the station in Tampa, Mel Tillis called and we had lunch together. I learned a lot from Mel that day. At that time, he owned a couple of radio stations over in the Pensacola and Mobile area. Many years later, when Carol and I visited Mel at his Branson, Missouri, theater, we had a nice visit reminiscing about all our past activities and shows. I also learned he was a Gator at heart, having gone to the University of Florida.

I received a call one day from a woman identifying herself as

Tammy. Surprised, I said, "Who?" She replied, "Who, hell, yore feet don't fit no limb. This is Tammy Wynette." Seems she and George Jones had just gotten married and were moving to Florida near Tampa, where later they were opening up their own theater.

I guess the first show we promoted in the new coliseum in 1961 had lit a little fire under me. From 1961 until 1984, when I held my last concert, I had probably promoted over seventy-five to a hundred concerts. Some of the stars who came year after year were Ray Price, Sunny James, Waylon Jennings, Willie Nelson, Ferlin Husky, Faron Young, George Jones, Tammy Wynette, Jean Shepherd, and Connie Smith. The Gatlin Brothers were always crowd-pleasers, as was Jack Green. Jim Ed Brown was a favorite along with Jan Howard and Jeannie Sealey, and there are many more who from memory I cannot recall.

Backstage at a concert Jack Greene chats with Bobby and me

I learned from hobnobbing with these folks backstage, and many times even out on their buses, how they lived and much about their personal lives and their families. A love of country music came through from each of them, as much as mine or more so.

Over the years, Ray Price was by far my biggest-selling country-music star. I felt when I had him on the lineup, which I did almost every year, I could go to the bank and borrow money. That's how much confidence I had in his ticket sales. Behind him came Ferlin Husky, Charley Pride, Mel Tillis, and Sunny James. When you booked Ferlin Husky, you got two stars for the price of one, because he always did his Simon Crum act on the stage. Tom T. Hall was another top ticket-seller for me.

Grandpa Jones and me reminiscing

By far the biggest show I ever promoted came in February 1971. Sometime in November 1970, I had received a call from an agent named Jack Johnson. He had heard about me promoting shows, and he had a great lineup for me. I said, "Tell me about it." He had a blind piano player named Ronnie Milsap for $400, a little girl singer named Crystal Gayle for $400, and the star was Charley Pride for $2,000.

I immediately stopped him. I was not interested. Charley Pride was black, and even though we played his records, I just wasn't sure that people were ready for him. I could even visualize a protest march with people out in front of the coliseum. Mr. Johnsons replied, "You don't understand. People love him, and we've been selling out everywhere we've been."

I was still reluctant, because the civil-rights movement was in full swing, and I felt it was too big of a gamble for me place everything I had—my radio stations—on the line by promoting a Negro in those days of 1971. After two weeks, Mr. Johnson called me again and asked if I had thought any more about the show. I told him I was going to pass on it. In that case, he said, "I'll bring the show to your towns and buy a few spots on your radio station."

After thinking for a moment, I said, "Hold on and let me get back to you tomorrow." I talked to Frank and my brother Bob. I talked with my managers in Macon and in Tampa. They all agreed that I was overly cautious and that I should go ahead with the show. I called the man back and told him I had changed my mind, and let's go with the show. The talent was to cost $2,800 a night for three nights.

An added plus for this show happened when my brother Bob started with the morning show while I was recuperating from an auto accident. He called himself "Rapid Robert." One morning, he asked if it would be all right if he played a few cuts from a talking comedy record he had already been playing a few cuts off of. Our listeners seemed to really like it for variety. At first I was hesitant, but after listening to the down-home fellow's humor, who could resist? It was an LP by a fertilizer salesman from Mississippi named Jerry Clower, and it was recorded on Lemon Records. For the next few days, Bob played more of his talking comedy releases from the album, and every day it seemed we got more and more phone calls. His Mississippi-type humor of "Knock him out, John," and so on was really catching ears in our area.

After seeing the response, I got a bright idea and told my secretary, Frieda Prince, to try to get in touch with Mr. Clower and tell him we'll send him an airplane ticket and get him a hotel room if he'd like to come to Jacksonville and Tampa and be on the show with Charley Pride and the others. But he would have to travel to Jacksonville and Tampa, so see if he could work it in his fertilizer-sales schedule.

One of America's favorite country stars and songwriters, Mel Tillis backstage before a performance

Saturday night, he was backstage in the Jacksonville coliseum wearing a bright yellow suit. I introduced him to Jack Johnson, Charley Pride's manager, and said he was going to be on the show with us. Mr. Johnson said "No, he is not—this is a union show, and he is not a member." Embarrassed, I turned to Jerry Clower and said, "The show starts at eight p.m. How about going out and warming up the crowd while they are coming in and finding their seats?" He did, and he wowed them, yelling his jokes about Marcel Ledbetter and Yazoo City for over thirty minutes.

Charley watched him tell his down-home Mississippi jokes from backstage, and the next night in Tampa, he put his arm around Jerry, introducing him to the crowd saying, "This is my new friend, I want y'all to meet and welcome Jerry Clower." The rest is history, and I was happy to see Jerry wrote about me and this event in his book, *Ain't God Great*. I was later invited to appear with him onstage in Macclenny and Waycross.

When booking a show in back in the '60s, '70s, or early '80s, you could usually count on the building or venue expenses costing about 10 percent of your gross. That would cover the ticket sales, police, and insurance. That show with Charley Pride turned out to be the most profitable concert I ever had, and probably the greatest promotion of my life. In Macon, we grossed over $39,000, the next night in Jacksonville over $42,000, and on Sunday in Tampa over $37,000. And to think I was reluctant to bring Charley Pride to our area!

Before 1961 when the city of Jacksonville built the coliseum, we promoted several shows in the old Duval County Armory. One time we promoted a New Year's Eve dance with Hank Snow and his band. He was the only star I could get when I called my agent in Nashville. I guess I was so anxious to have a New Year's Eve event that I didn't stop to realize that people could not dance to his style of music, such as "I'm Moving On."

Another show we had in the Armory during that period

featured Carl Smith and June Carter. That was before Carl married Goldie Hill. On the show, June Carter kept calling Carl an old knothead. One day, Frank and I were talking about it, and I thought that name was different, so Frank hung it on me for many years to come, sometimes calling me Knothead Boss.

Another show in the old Duval County Armory that we promoted was Bob Wills and the Texas Playboys, featuring Lefty Frizzell. Their music left me spellbound, with horns and drums and twin guitars and fiddle players. Plus I fell in love with Lefty's type of singing, such as "If You've Got the Money, I've Got the Time," "The Mom and Dad's Waltz," and many other hits.

During my career, I only had two disappointing events or near failures. On one occasion, I had booked Johnny Cash and June Carter in the Civic Auditorium on Bay Street in Jacksonville on a Friday night, and the only venue available for the Saturday-night event was the Orlando City Auditorium. After hearing some disturbing news about Johnny Cash's personal life, I decided to go ahead with the event anyway and paid the country-music radio station in Orlando $3,500 to front it and promote it heavily. On the air, it was to be "their" show. For the two-night event, I added Tex Ritter and Jimmy C. Newman.

Things went well in Jacksonville on Friday night, even though I noticed Johnny Cash was pawing like a raving bull while backstage waiting to go on. That worried me, because I had never seen a person acting as strange as he was backstage. The next night, things were not so pleasant. The first show in the Orlando Auditorium went off without a hitch. However, Johnny Cash did not show up for the second show. When it came time for him to go on, I announced to a packed house that he was not to be found, and if anyone wanted their money back go to the front box office now. To my knowledge, no one wanted their money back, because Tex Ritter, Jimmy C. Newman, and June Carter put on a great show anyhow.

The big problem came the following week, when the radio station in Orlando threatened to sue me. I had my attorney call them, and they backed off. After all, it was not my fault. I never forgot that night, and even though Johnny Cash would later become an even bigger star, I never used him again on any of our shows. The show was held prior to Johnny Cash and June Carter marrying, which undoubtedly made a change in his life.

The other failure of a concert I had promoted was when I was convinced by my agent to bring Charlie Rich to Jacksonville and any other auditorium in Florida that might be available. He was red-hot with songs like "Behind Closed Doors" and "The Most Beautiful Girl" and several others, and he would really sell tickets. I went to work and set the date in Jacksonville for a Friday night, but the only auditorium in Florida for the next night on Saturday was the Miami Beach Auditorium. After going to Miami and talking to the country-music station there, I decided to go on with the show. After all, it was only about three or four months after the Charley Pride show, and I guess I was still feeling my oats from that success.

Thank heaven that on the show with Charlie Rich we had scheduled a relative newcomer, Waylon Jennings, plus Ronnie Milsap and one other female vocalist. After heavily promoting the show in Jacksonville and spending about $3,000 with the Miami country-music station, on the morning of the event I received a call from my agent in Nashville saying Charlie Rich had canceled at the last moment and would not be there. The agent had lined up some substitute artists if I wanted them.

I declined to add any more expenses to the show. Waylon Jennings would be our star, and he was there wearing a tuxedo. On the night of the show, before the performance began, I told the Miami Beach audience twice that Charlie Rich would not be there, and if they wanted their money back to go up front and get it now. To my knowledge, no one left. However, during the following week, my bookkeeper wrote out over $1,000 in checks refunding the damn transplanted Yankees in Miami their money. *Never again*, I thought, and I vowed to look more closely at the character of my future stars or artists that I would bring to town. For that and other reasons, I never booked Jerry Lee Lewis but once, feeling he was a little bit too raunchy onstage for the image we wanted at our country-music festivals.

Although I personally chose, signed up, and promoted most of the country-music shows that came to Jacksonville, once in a while an artist or his agent would call and ask me to participate in a one-night event. This usually happened when an artist had several dates scheduled within driving time and wanted to fill a particular date.

One such event was when Merle Haggard's manager called me about a date in the middle of the week. I was a little reluctant and told him so, because all of our country shows had either been on Friday or Saturday night and we usually had several acts on a WQIK-promoted concert. Merle's manager and I struck a deal whereby Merle would work for a percentage of the ticket sales. This Thursday-night show was the only night open for Merle, and he was the only act to perform in this concert event.

We went ahead with the show in the Jacksonville Civic Auditorium. Haggard and his band put on a fantastic show for over two hours to a packed house. I received many calls and letters later telling about how great it was. It seems the acoustics or sound was much better in the Civic Auditorium, and people loved it.

Just before the show finished, Merle's manager, Fuzzy Owens, and I went into the front office at the Civic Auditorium and settled up with the money from tickets sales. He asked me to walk out to the big beautiful bus they were traveling in, and I wondered why. He went around to the back of the bus, took out a special key, and opened a secret compartment just above the engine in the rear. When he opened the door, a light came on inside, and I could see perhaps thirty or forty paper bags crammed full of cash money.

I thought it was very interesting because on each paper bag he would write the date, the time, the amount, and the weather for the event. I thought to myself, *What a way to keep books on Haggard's performances while they were traveling.* After all, his take for that night in Jacksonville alone was over $8,000. If the rest of those paper bags had that much money or more, there was a lot of cash in that little cubbyhole located in the back of the bus.

CHAPTER 7

FAMILY MATTERS

As I approach the latter years of my life and write this book, my wife has been gone for over a year and a half. Each day I am still eager to move on, to make new friends, and with the enthusiasm I got back at the dairy when I was only twelve years old, I decided to give this book my best shot and fill it with my lifetime of adventures. Having shared so many of my radio and country-music stories, I don't want to neglect the other very important part of my life, my wife and family.

During our fifty-seven years together, Carol and I had a good marriage—in fact, one of the best. We had very few quarrels, and as I look back over the years, it was probably because she always went along with most anything I wanted to do, although I would have to convince her first that it was in our best interests. Like many couples, our marriage had many ups and downs, but the ups far exceeded the downs.

Carol guided our children in their manners, their dress, and their religious activities, as well as all the basics they needed as they grew up. About all the boys got from me was, "Don't be afraid of hard work." Many times over, I would tell them, "Don't worry about the mule, just load the wagon," or maybe, "Dammitt, get out of the house and go have fun."

Though it was not to be, my wife always wanted a girl—maybe because our sons were always getting into trouble, as young boys will do. Many times at dinner, after my wife would prepare a wonderful meal, she would leave the table because the boys and I became so raucous. Today I love my four sons and their families, and I appreciate them more than ever since my wife passed away. But I've always remembered: boys will be boys.

From the day I married Carol, I really felt she wanted me to build our first radio station or business and settle in that particular town for the rest of our lives. It didn't happen; we seemed to move every four or five years. We built and lived in three houses in Fernandina Beach. We lived in South Jacksonville and in the Deerwood area for many years. At one time, we had a beautiful home on the river across from downtown Jacksonville. And we lived in Tampa, Florida, for two years. We finally settled in St. Augustine, where we lived for eighteen years. Thank heaven when she bought furniture for our homes she always bought good quality, because we surely needed it in all our moving around. I have to say that every time we moved and sold our house, we usually made a profit, and it would go into our next home.

Perhaps my biggest and most expensive weakness over the years was for boats, cars, and a new pickup truck for myself almost every year. Even today, my friends and my children tease me about the trucks and cars I have owned. My friends say they never know what I'll drive up in when I visit them.

At one time, while operating WQIK, I had an association with a Ford dealer in Folkston, Georgia. During that time, I supplied my wife with a new car every year and sometimes a new truck for myself twice a year. When I was a kid, I'd always wanted my own pickup truck, and I still have one today.

I love boats and boating. From my first boat in 1950 to the present day, I have owned twenty or more, ranging in size from a twelve-foot skiff to a forty-five-foot Hatteras and even a forty-eight-foot houseboat at one time. I love the water, plus traveling all over Florida and the Bahamas with my family was a time of real relaxation and enjoyment for me.

While on one of our many boats, I would sleep like a log from the slight rocking motion while moored on the water. I'm not a good swimmer—my lifetime of asthma limits my breathing ability—but cramming our family of boys aboard one of our boats for either a weekend outing or a two- or three-week vacation was always a great time for my wife and I. We must have spent over twenty summers vacationing aboard one of our crafts in the pristine waters of the Bahamas. But in time, all these wonderful family outings and good-time trips with our family would come to a halt.

Carol and me weighing in a big fish

While we were living in St. Augustine in July 2002, on a routine family visit to our doctor at Mayo, I mentioned that Carol was getting very forgetful and was doing things like leaving the lights or the coffeepot turned on and constantly losing or misplacing things. After spending some time with her, our family doctor, Dr. Hill McBrayer, told me that Carol had some kind of dementia that was in its early stages. Later in 2004, when her forgetfulness and her memory problems had gotten much worse, I again took her to Mayo, only this time to the main clinic in Jacksonville. There, after a day-and-a-half examination, she was formally diagnosed with Alzheimer's. In private conversations, I was told to make certain she took her medicine; it would not cure the Alzheimer's but would slow it down and keep her safe.

It was during this time, while staying at home with Carol, that I began to try to learn to play the piano. I also got out my old Rickenbacker steel guitar and started playing it for myself for the first time since 1957. I played around the house and then later, as a hobby, I began making steel guitars with my own design in my garage workshop. That was about all I had to occupy my time while keeping an eye on her.

At some time during that period, I met a fellow named J. C. Hunnicutt who invited me to come over to his friend's house and play with his group for fun. I did, and Carol went with me on several occasions until she became too ill. We both enjoyed those outings of playing country music, although she would get very nervous after an hour or two.

The final years from 2008 until her death in March 2012 were really rough. Up until September 2010, I would stay with my wife 95 percent of the time. She simply did not want anyone to stay with her other than our housekeeper, Irena, or me. I was told by a lady with the Council on Aging for St. Johns County that I should go home and begin "divorcing" myself from my wife, because it was only going to get worse. *Never*, I thought, and I said the same to my son Stephen, who was at the meeting with me. On several occasions, one of our sons would come to St. Augustine and stay with her or take her out to dinner or just for a ride somewhere.

One morning when I was driving alone up to Georgia, having left Carol with Irena, I suddenly realized that my life would never be the same again. That thought hit me like a bolt out of the blue, and I began to cry uncontrollably. I pulled my truck off the road and parked, and there all alone in my vehicle, I sobbed my heart out and prayed to God. To see a beautiful person's mind get worse and worse year after year is really heartbreaking. I tried to get professional help to come to our house, but each time my wife would fight it off, telling me that the aides were stealing her jewelry and not feeding her and such.

Relaxing with our winning Blue Marlin
(I wanted to hug its neck but it had none)

From 2009 until her final days, all she talked about were her childhood days back in St. Marys, Georgia, and that's when I decided to put our home on the water in St. Augustine up for sale and move her into her old family homestead in St. Marys, which we had owned from the early '70s. It had been remodeled and was comfortable. We moved there in March of 2010, and just a few months later in September 2010, my sons and I all agreed it was time for me to let go and start looking for a home where she would get twenty-four-hour-a-day care.

Living through the last years of a person's life who has Alzheimer's disease and seeing my soulmate and partner of many years slowly deteriorate was like a flashback to the day my mother was taken from me when I was less than four years old—an event that haunts me to this day. In September 2010, we placed Carol in a nursing home in south Jacksonville. On the last day of February 2012, she fell, and after five days in the hospital she was taken to a hospice, where she died on March 12, 2012.

She has gone home to her beloved St. Marys, where she is buried along with her mother and father and the other Casey members. At her funeral, our good friend Rev. Gene Zimmerman spoke these words: "Today there's another angel in heaven." I agree with him, even as that statement brought a closure to our fifty-eight years of happiness.

Being with a spouse and seeing her die from Alzheimer's leaves a lasting impression on a person and is something no one should have to go through, but many will. Hopefully someday there'll be a cure for Alzheimer's.

Before she died, my wife told some of her lady friends that she wanted Marshall to go on with his happy-go-lucky lifestyle after she was gone. In those days, it seemed as if life's realities were hitting me hard right square in the face. My wife had died and, only five weeks earlier, my only living brother Bobby had died in the hospital in Cocoa Beach, Florida.

The latter years of my life have been very different than I ever thought about in my younger years. They say the older years are the golden years, but I must tell you, I disagree. Looking back and thinking about the early years, the most wonderful day of my life was the day in July 1954 when a young lady right out of college appeared at WJHP. She was applying for a job. She was dressed immaculately. I was busy in a nearby studio filing phonograph records from my morning show, but I noticed her sitting out front waiting for the manager for her interview. I remember strolling out into the front lobby and asking the receptionist if I had any phone calls of importance.

At that time, I was one of the top disc jockeys with the morning show in Jacksonville. I couldn't help but eyeballing the young lady sitting, waiting for her interview. She was beautiful in a simple way. Right off, I was smitten by her. My memories of her coming to work at the radio station and later our dating and finally our marriage will never leave me.

The memories of my wife and children and hundreds of vacations together all over the eastern part of the United States and the Bahamas also will never leave me. Early in the 1960s, when I first bought a boat, and for the years up until the year 2000, we would take vacations to the Bahamas or the Keys, or just spend weekends on it in the North Florida area. Cramming our entire family on a thirty-six-foot boat was no easy task, but Carol always handled it so that we never missed a meal.

We really enjoyed those vacations, especially when we caught some fish, or Brian brought up lobster from the bottom of the ocean. These memories will be with me forever. Indeed, these are treasures, and to me memories are valuable gifts one has when he reaches my age, with the lifetime I have been honored to have.

Today, as I look back on my career of playing country music, building and operating radio stations, and promoting country-music concerts, I imagine people tend to think of me as a wealthy individual. Not so, but I am comfortable, just as I had always hoped I'd wind being in with my life. Over the years, in accomplishing what I have, I probably sweated out more payrolls than John D.

Rockefeller or Henry Ford ever did. The big problem with being in the public eye with any FCC-licensed utility sanctioned by the government is that the sale price makes media headlines, but dang it, the media won't tell you how much a person or company owes when it was sold, not in bold headlines anyway. In short, I probably made as many bad financial decisions as I did good ones. When I was a youngster, I simply had it too easy with making money, and I guess I thought it would never end. It did.

So where am I today? I have invested heavily in land south of my hometown of Brunswick, Georgia, and I have enough in the bank to comfortably retire on if I don't get above my raisin's, as the old saying goes. Today I am at peace with the world, but most of all at the age of eighty-two I am in good health, which money cannot buy. And let me not forget, I have a bunch of young-uns, six grand young-uns, and two great grand young-uns who love me.

People often ask me why I would name my autobiography *Fertilizer 'tween My Toes*. It's because I shoveled tons of cow manure or fertilizer cleaning out the barns and loading that old John Deere tractor with it when I was twelve through sixteen years old. Those were the learning years of my life. Pete and Noody Gibson taught me more about life and dealing with people than I learned in school. Basically, they and their mother taught me right from wrong. But the good part of it all is, I'm just as happy to be alive today as I was back then. And to me, that's what life is all about—being happy yourself, and making others you come in daily contact with happy also.

As I enter the final phase of my life, I do so without my beloved wife, Carol. She was the solid rock beside me. Sometimes it's hard to be enthusiastic about your future when you reach the age of eighty-two all alone, but that's life. As my son Stephen would say, "It is what it is." But I have to remember, I had only ten years of schooling, and it's only in America that a country boy with my background could attain the success, friendship, and love that I have acquired in my lifetime.

(L-R) Phil Niekro (Pitcher for the Atlanta Braves), Jerry Clower, Pete Gibson (my old boss at the Dairy), Neil Linton, Mayor Jake Godbold, Mae Axton, Me, Frank Thies, Henry Cook (my caricature artist), Country music star Bobby Bare, Glenn Reeves, Suzanne Cato, Joe Niekro

As I look around our nation today and see how things are changing, I have often said I'm glad I lived when I did. I am convinced the United States would be better off today if some of our leaders got some of my fertilizer 'tween their toes. I play or practice on my steel guitar almost every day either by myself or with a group, and as I have told my group and friends many times, the day it ceases to be fun is the day I quit.

Writing an autobiography at my age without assistance is no easy task. For several months I have researched, talked with many people including my family and others, and spent many hours alone in deep thought about the events I have witnessed during my life. No doubt about it, I have been the most blessed man you'll read or hear about on earth today, as you'll discover in my memoirs.

Today more than ever in my lifetime, I treasure the love of my family. Among my most valued memories are the gatherings we held many times a year. Spending Easter holidays, Thanksgivings, Christmas, birthdays, along with trips on our boat to the Bahamas—all of these and many more have brought us together for the good times I never experienced during my childhood. Here we are together, posing for Christmas at sometime in the mid-2000s.

My entire family enjoying a Christmas get together in 2005

Besides my wife Carol and I, shown above are my sons Marty (Marshall Jr.), with his wife, Vicky, and two daughters, Jacque and Casey; Rick, with his wife, Erika, and their two daughters, Chloe

116

and Mary; Brian, with his wife, Kim, and their family, Marlena and Hannah; and Stephen, the youngest. They are my legacy, far more than any material items like owning a radio station, promoting a concert, or any other events or things I have talked of in this, the story of my life.